THE SEARCH BOOK:

A Guide to Executive Selection

❦

Donn F. Vickers
Cindy Hilsheimer

❦

Table of Contents

Foreword

This book is especially for board members—those open-hearted, open-handed folks who do so much to guard, guide, and make good the missions of our nonprofit organizations. When you signed up for board service you probably did not know it would also include executive search. Now here you are with an unexpected task, a limited budget, and already more than enough to do.

It is that coming together of less-than-happy conditions that caused us to assemble this small book. The "us" in this case is far more than the two of us at the bottom of this page. It is our colleagues and friends on the editorial advisory committee who as board members and executives have lived through this search process which now you face. While they do have the very last word here (see Afterwords II), they also had the very first word with us about the substance and shape of what follows. That is to say this is largely a collection of our combined wisdom.

The first three chapters are addressed to you as board members. They are designed to help you get a perspective on your executive transition, assess the present status and special needs of your organization, and create a profile of the kind of leadership all that suggests.

Most of Chapter IV and all of Chapter V tackle the selection and specific work of the search committee, and thus these sections are intended as a guide for search committee members in addition to boards. We could have ended with Chapter VI on the details of checking out, contracting with, and celebrating your selected finalist for the position. We didn't. We believe that the entry attitudes and behaviors of the new executive and board are so crucial that we added a Chapter VII, "The First 100 Days," addressed to the new executive in addition to the board.

Our hope is that much of what is on these pages will be of assistance with this unexpected task, making it far easier and more affordable. If that is so you can join with us in appreciation to Elfi Di Bella and the good people at Huntington National Bank for their sponsorship. Thanks as well to Margaret Wildi and Grange Insurance for their always-professional printing job.

Finally, though, foremost on our appreciation list is Kelly Stevelt Kaser, the talented and trusted colleague at the Academy for Leadership & Governance. Her initial good work of research and final work of preparing the manuscript were as always exemplary. Our editor, Karen Simonian, made smooth the language and clear the sentences in a way that makes us all proud.

Donn F. Vickers
Cindy Hilsheimer
Columbus, Ohio
Summer, 2007

Chapter I

Getting a Perspective on the Transition

You did not ask for it. You did not sign up for it. But here it is, and you are on the board and there is no ducking it. Further, you just may be a board member who has relied heavily on your executive, and now the ease and comfort of that reliance is disappearing. Now what? What do you need to know and what will you need to be prepared to do during this executive transition?

In what follows we will take you through five propositions that won't answer all the questions, but perhaps will begin to create an approach, a foundation upon which to build the important details of your executive search. Here they are in summary:

It is to be expected. While perhaps not a matter of great solace, in the world of nonprofit work, you can generally count on a change in executive leadership about every six to eight years.

It will require leadership. Most likely the leadership required for the search and the ongoing work of the organization will now come to you as a board member more than ever before.

It will take time and resources. This will not be a simple and swift four to six week process with no new budget expense.

It must not displace the work. The work, of course, is the ongoing program and service of your organization. You need to be prepared to make sure it goes forward in a reliable and quality way.

It can be a gift. While it probably won't feel like it in the beginning, with any luck the notion that it is far more a burden than a blessing will change. Some very good and new things can happen.

That is the summary statement. Here is a bit more to help you think about and get ready for this important work of executive search.

It Is To Be Expected

It is true that some executives stay in their position with a particular organization for more than 20 years. It is also true that they do so with continued energy and creativity and with full support of their boards. This is not the norm. An excellent study by the Illinois Arts Alliance published in 2003 indicated that 70% of the executives surveyed intended to leave their jobs within the next five years. That was in arts agencies and that was Illinois. But just in case you might blame that turnover on the executives or the character of artists, along comes a study on 2,000 nonprofit executives of all types in nine cities across the nation. This comprehensive look at executive leadership conducted by CompassPoint in 2006 indicated that 75% of those surveyed intended to leave their positions in the next five years.

Not just in the for-profit sector, but also in the nonprofit sector, turnover is a common, perhaps natural, and maybe unavoidable, fact of life. So, while you as a board member will likely not welcome it, what you are signing up for, if you sign up for a six-year term, is the likelihood of also signing up for an executive search. If you are particularly fond of your executive and wish to lessen that likelihood, there are some things you can do. Effective executive evaluation is surely one of them.

While regular, thoughtful executive evaluation does not ensure executive retention, the practice of regular evaluation and thoughtful conversation with your executive around expectations, focus, level of satisfaction, and quality of work may just strengthen the relationship between you and your executive in such a way as to increase the likelihood of a longer and more mutually gratifying tenure. We have written about this subject in more detail in *Evaluating Your Executive: New Approaches, New Purposes* (The Academy for Leadership & Governance, 2006).

In any case, while there are some things you can do as a board member to increase the chance that your executive will stay for a longer period of time, the odds are that he will move on in six to eight years to another opportunity, and you will need to prepare yourself for an executive search.

It Will Require Leadership

When the executive steps down the board needs to step up. That is probably dependable and good advice. The question remains: What does it mean to step up, to take wider and greater responsibility?

Some would say that the primary issue here is who will drive the transition and search period and process. For some, the answer is that it should be board-driven; for others, that it should be consultant-driven; and still others, that it should be search firm-driven. Depending on your budget, ability and confidence, you may decide one way or another. Because you, as board members, are the ones who must decide indicates that, even with a consultant or search firm, the board must lead, stay engaged, even stay fully and finally in charge of the process.

There are excellent consultants who can help, and there are reputable search firms who do good work for nonprofits. Our belief is that many boards, given the right kind of assistance, can and should do the work of executive search. And, for many boards—the majority in fact—with budgets of $500,000 and less, the cost of the consultant or search firm makes them not a reasonable alternative. And so, we have created this small book with which we intend to make it possible for you to do the work of the executive search. If done in an orderly and effective manner it will likely produce a satisfying result for you at a moderate cost of time and a very little cost of money.

Your own board leadership during this period will vary a bit, depending upon why it is you need a new executive. For the majority it will come about because your board president, over lunch, will find out that your executive director plans to resign to take a different job or to retire. With luck, the "notice" given is three months or more in advance of the planned departure, the leaving is amicable, and you will have time to celebrate the contribution of your executive and outline a plan for the search.

Better yet, your board may be operating under a succession plan adopted 18 months ago that contains not only the likely time of departure, but the details of position description, interim leadership, and timetable and details for the search for a new executive. This "in-advance" leadership on the part of the board is, of course, the best-case situation and lays the groundwork for the kind of healthy executive separation, search, and selection we'd all hope for.

A more challenging situation for your leadership would present itself if you had a history of an all-volunteer organization and were moving toward acquiring your first part- or full-time paid executive. In this regard you will face two big leadership challenges, and both brand-new: first, deciding upon and finding the kind of executive you need, and second, changing your organizational culture to accommodate the dual leadership of board *and* staff.

Perhaps the most challenging set of circumstances would be that you have had to ask your present executive to leave. The pain and difficulty of that will probably not be alleviated by knowing that the CompassPoint study previously alluded to claims that one-third of the present executives reported that their predecessors were "fired or pushed out." While that, at first, seems somewhat shocking and certainly unfortunate, the context must include what we read about for-profit CEO experience and what we know of other partnerships, which continue to fail at a near 50% rate. The point here is that, with this kind of departure, far more is required and needed from board leadership. That would, no doubt, include attention to potential legal matters and special sensitivity to the staff, board, and constituent relationships.

In sum, whatever amount of leadership you and your board colleagues have shared with your executive in the past, most, if not all, of that will change during this transition. At this important, even critical time, a different and more expanded version of your leadership will be required. It may require a retreat or outside consultation to get you prepared. It will certainly require extra time and renewed commitment to the life and mission of your organization. You will not want to exclude your executive as you move into the transition period, but you will want to move forward, taking full charge of the process. You and your fellow board members are the ones who will remain and be holding in trust the mission of your organization. In short, as the executive begins to step down you will need to step up to a fuller kind of leadership that takes a fuller kind of responsibility for the well-being of your organization.

It Will Take Time and Resources

Here's the good news. You are not in the for-profit sector involved in a CEO search where, according to *Harper's Magazine* (December, 2005), the average amount spent on each search is $2 million. And, perhaps worse, the chance that the CEO will quit or be fired within 18 months is one in two.

Here's what you can count on: a search period of four to six months and perhaps as long as eight or nine months. Our experience is that this is one of those places where haste does make waste. The hurry-up-and-get-it-done approach often results in not getting it quite right and, further in, having to do it again. Perhaps the most important advice to pass on to you at this juncture, as you get ready for the action steps of the search, is to prepare yourself to take it easy, work thoughtfully through the steps of the process, and schedule a celebration for having done it well with good results.

Speaking of the steps in the process, Chapters II through VII will present lots of details on each of those steps. For now, here is a preview outline of what you might expect to do and the number of weeks each might take. We say "might" because with a small committee and all the right circumstances it may take less time.

Sample Timeline for Executive Search

Activity	Time Assigned	Cumulative Weeks
Board Organizational Assessment	2 Weeks	
Board Outline of Position Profile	2 Weeks	4 Weeks
Board Identifies and Recruits Search Committee	2 Weeks	6 Weeks
Search Committee Orientation to Board's Assignment and Assessments	1 Week	7 Weeks
Search Committee Utilizes Various Methods to Attract a Pool of Qualified Applicants	2 Weeks	9 Weeks
Applications Sent and Received with Résumés	3 Weeks	12 Weeks
Applications Reviewed and eight to 10 Finalists Selected	1 Week	13 Weeks
Telephone Interviews Conducted	1 Week	14 Weeks
Three to Five Candidates Selected and Interviewed	1 Week	15 Weeks
Second Interviews and Reference Checks with two to three Candidates	2 Weeks	17 Weeks
Finalist Chosen and Presented, and Contract Negotiated	2 Weeks	19 Weeks
Plan Devised and Implemented to Orient New Executive and Establish Goals and Expectations for the first "100 days"	3 Weeks	22 Weeks

Thanks to Sheila Albert and her dependably useful book, *Hiring the Chief Executive* (BoardSource, 2000), for the suggestion of a timeline in chart form.

Depending on the season of the year and the availability of board and search committee members, the previous sample timeline might need to be expanded. From our perspective, implementing these steps more quickly would be difficult to do.

On the issue of resources you may wish to consider a list of the following potential expenses:

Printing various fact sheets, applications, and organization descriptions	$300 to $1,000
Communications: postage and long-distance phone service	$100 to $300
Travel and per diem for three to five candidates	$1,200 to $2,400
Second interviews with two to three candidates	$900 to $1,800
Miscellaneous hospitality and other costs	$500 to $1,000
Total	**$3,000 to $6,500**

Note: The above is computed for an organization with a $500,000 to $1 million budget with all volunteer assistance and no professional fee.

It Must Not Displace the Work

If your search, from beginning to end, takes six months, the organization cannot take a six-month leave of absence. In the early part of the search, during the organizational assessment, description of the position, and recruitment and selection of the search committee, you and your colleague board members will be putting in extra hours. This will diminish the number of extra hours available to keep the organization moving forward, delivering programs, and doing the necessary fundraising and marketing to support them.

There are some short-term staffing solutions. Some organizations appoint a senior staff member as acting director during the period of the search. Others have chosen to select a seasoned (sometimes retired) board member to act as executive, for up to a six-month period. It is possible that some portion of, or all of, the executive committee be assigned to conduct a quasi-administrative staffing function. The goal in any of these is to ensure that the work plan gets implemented and the organization continues to do its work during the necessary time required for the search process.

Some organizations, in fact, have adjusted their work and program output during executive search. One consolidated two of its programs into one in order to save time and resources. Another added some training time to staff meetings to broaden the scope and abilities of what each staff person was able to do. Still another put one of its long-time programs on "sabbatical" for a year and utilized half or less of the time to carry out a much-needed evaluation and also negated the need to raise funds for the effort. The point is to keep your organization healthy and producing during an extended transition period. The work of the search is of crucial importance, but you and the board must guard against it becoming the primary work. The transition seems to work better for all purposes when it does not consume the creative leadership energies and efforts of the board. The mission continues to be the organizational mission and the program goals continue to be the primary responsibility of the life of the organization. In short, Search with focus and vigor and, as well, maintain the focus and vigor of the organization.

It Can Be a Gift

The news that you are losing your executive will not feel good. The news that you are losing a beloved and very effective executive will feel even worse. But even in the latter case, the time without an executive, and the process of the executive search, can come to be experienced as a gift.

One of our colleagues suggested that it was his observation that many organizations were at their strongest during a transition period without an executive. Many board members grasped, for the first time, the notion that it truly was their organization. Others, who were previously not involved, suddenly found that they were needed to keep the organizational ship afloat. We all, of course, hope for these kinds of things, with or without an executive. If a transition without one brings them on, we can be grateful for that gift.

Sometimes, during a transition, there is an opportunity to focus on things we otherwise might neglect with a "full steam ahead executive." The transition period presents a good time to clarify and examine anew the organization's systems, structures, staffing, and finances. Many organizations, run by a strong executive, rely too much on the sheer will and energy of that executive. As a result things like systems, structures, and staffing are often loose to informal. One organization decided that the transition was a good time to rewrite position descriptions as a way of better defining the work of the staff. Another organization reworked the structure and responsibility of board committees and chairs. Another involved an enlarged fund development committee to review and assess all the sources of funding and decide on some new strategies that included a greater number of board members. This stabilization process is key work because it lays important groundwork for the new executive leadership. This re-examination of systems and procedures is important work because it lays important groundwork for the new executive leadership.

You may wish to put in place certain ritual celebrations during the transition period. For many they seem to be an important aspect of marking the departure of a founder and the arrival of a new executive. You, as a board, need to determine what is a natural fit for your organization—the degree of formality and fun, the extent to which you will merge the personal and the professional.

Consider who it is that needs to say goodbye to the founding director in a celebratory way. You may decide to go beyond the board and close constituents to the broader community. When that seems like the right path to take, you may want to create another setting for the "immediate family" of the organization. It is for you to determine what is the best mix of celebration and tribute, of written and oral communications, of mementos and gifts. It will be a major passage for your organization, and it will likely feel more completed and concluded if you pay attention to some rituals in which those important to your organization can participate.

In short, positive benefits can come to your organization unexpectedly as a result of an executive transition—if you are paying proper attention and taking proper action. Be on the lookout for these gifts.

Chapter II

The Board Gets Clear: Assessing the Organization

This chapter is about getting a clear picture of yourself as an organization before inviting someone new into it. We find that one of the benefits of being without an executive and needing to do the work of the executive search is the necessity to pause and reflect on your organization—not usually a thing most of us do in the regular and breathless pace of organizational life. It can be a satisfying and strengthening exercise for the board leadership of your organization. In the case of executive search it can provide clarity and potency to the language you use to speak about your organization, not only to potential executive candidates, but to all those who might refer strong candidates to you.

To assist you with your organizational self-assessment, we offer six ways for you to clarify who you are before proceeding to determine who it is you want. Our guess is that you will not want to pause long enough to think about it in all six ways. Our hope is that you will choose the two or three ways that seem to provide the most likely routes into your present organizational identity. Our belief is that the ones that produce the most energy for lively board discussion will be the ones with the most promise of establishing a strong foundation for your executive search.

In order to get you started, we have provided an outline and short description of the six self- assessment exercises. Since you know your situation best, you will know which ones best fit. You will also know whether to utilize them as part of two or three regular board meetings or at a special retreat-like setting of your board. Don't overdo or overwork. Likewise too little time is more apt to lead to the feeling of merely going through the paces and producing not much of consequence.

So here are the six ideas to help you decide where to start:

1. **First Thoughts, Best Instincts.** Even without a whole lot of questions and extensive inventories, most of you have an instinctive sense about your organization. Capture that first. Permit and encourage board members to offer their own observations in an open, random way without constraints or structure.

2. **Our Distinctive Mission.** If you have just written a mission statement you may wish to skip this one. If not, and particularly if you can't recite it or even locate where it is written, this may be the place to start. What special cause got you started as an organization? What central purposes keep you going?

3. **Our Present Stage of Development.** Organizations, like people, tend to go through life stages. Each stage has its own characteristic challenges and, therefore, its own special leadership requirements. If you sense you are on the verge of a new stage, or stuck in an old one, this may be useful to you.

4. **The Culture of Our Organization.** Even relatively young organizations rather quickly establish habits and ways of doing business that can become powerful. Culture is to organizations what personality is to people. This may be a useful choice for you if you sense that much goes unexamined and too much is predictable in your organization.

5. **Our Primary Organizational Challenges.** The leader you select will no doubt be with you for five to eight years. What are the big issues and the likely problems she will confront? The number and intensity of the challenges you identify may very well have a bearing on just who it is you want with you when you confront those issues.

6. **The Environment in Which We Serve.** Scan everything from the economy of your town or city, to patterns of philanthropy and funding. Who in your community is doing something similar to you and what are the prospects for partnerships and collaboration? The first five exercises above offer an inside view. This last one focuses on the outside view and all the forces and opportunities that exist in your environment.

These are six windows through which to look to get a clearer view of your own organizational house. Board leaders: It is now up to you to select the two, three, or more that you believe will be the most helpful and then to find the time for your board to engage around them. In what follows we suggest ways of initiating and structuring your board conversations that could occur around each of the six.

First Thoughts, Best Instincts

Here are a couple of different ways this might work for you—the "all together around the table" way and the one-on-one way. The former could go like this. Ask all of the board members to get paper and pen to jot down for themselves what comes to mind around these questions: When you find yourself describing this organization to a friend or colleague at work, what do you say? When you talk about the most satisfying parts or your involvement, what words and phrases do you use? How about when you speak of the history of the organization? What about when you try to describe how it is evolving and changing? What makes you proudest? What do you worry about the most?

After five to ten minutes of note-taking around these questions, each member would share the most powerful description he jotted down in the course of responding to the questions. These would be recorded on a flip chart for all to see. When everyone had a chance to share, there would be a time of reflection on what was heard and a discussion about patterns of similarity, including words and phrases that were most often repeated. Those then would be pulled out and listed as the six to 10 most common impressions held about the present sense of the life of your organization.

Another way: Have board members divide into twos around the room. One board member would try to describe the organization to the other, who would take the role of someone who could potentially refer strong candidates to the organization for the executive search. The "referral" person would take notes on the characteristics of the organization that seemed most important when thinking about people to refer.

The board would then reassemble and record the notes describing the organization taken by the referral person. Once again, all the recorded notes would be reviewed for patterns of similarity and the most-mentioned items would be summarized and retained as the best first thoughts and instincts about the present characteristics of the organization.

Our Distinctive Mission

This exercise focuses on the "Big Picture." It will urge you to think more broadly than objectives, more general yet than goals, and it will be less tidy than most mission statements. The discussion of this section should put you back in touch with the initial energy and driving purpose which created your organization. It should, as well, link you to present enthusiasms and future visions.

The questions following are few in number, but they provide a good place for the thoughtful reflection that's so hard to come by in the usual round of organizational life.

- What was the special dream that launched our organization?
- How have we amended and enlarged that dream for this present situation?
- How can we imagine re-focusing the resources of this organization?
- What are we best at doing? What is our distinctive competence?
- For what are we valued in the community by its people and institutions?
- What is missing or goes poorly in our community if we are not here doing well?
- What do we find ourselves bragging about when we speak to friends about this organization?
- What is it now that we find ourselves getting most enthusiastic about?

Now having thought through these questions, what does any of this suggest about your selection of new leaders? That is the key question that will help you move from "who we are" to "what kind of leaders we want." The thoughtful discussion of these questions should lead you to better decisions.

Our Present Stage of Development

The calendar will tell you how old your organization is. It will not tell you what stage it is in. "Life cycle" implies an ongoing variety of organizational transitions. Where your organization is in its cycle does relate in an obvious way to leader choice. The stage you are moving toward requires special leader skills and sensitivities that differ from the stage you are departing. Most leaders have talents that better match one organizational life stage than another. Your job is to make a good match.

Organization life stages can be categorized in a variety of ways. The following chart lists five stages to assist you in assessing where you are, where you are likely to go, and what leadership skills are most important.

Organizational Stage	Leader Tasks and Traits
1. The initial dream	High creativity and commitment, flexibility, informal systems; the broad range of abilities of a generalist are needed.
2. Direction/consolidation	Organizational efficiency becomes primary; executive develops systems, policies, job descriptions; consolidates and formalizes the enterprise.
3. Expansion/diversification	Develops new projects; staff becomes semi-autonomous; the initial feel of a small "family business" is threatened; links with other institutions increase; generally more organizational complexity.
4. Coordination	Re-develops communication systems for new diversity; formalizes planning; defines implementation strategies, and methods and procedures for reporting.
5. Reformulation	Re-simplifies systems; restores central purpose; balances the variety of purposes and services.

Just as pre-adolescence is not altogether distinct from adolescence, neither is stage 2 distinct from 3 or 4 from 5. If you think about it, most often your organization is predominantly in one of the above stages. Since the stages tend to follow (not quite as night follows day), leader requirements for the next stage can be predicted with some accuracy. In short, leader selection will ideally match organizational stage.

The Culture of Our Organization

Culture is a lot of things that go together to make up the character of your organization. The items that follow will not be equal in importance to you. Some will produce a more useful discussion of your special culture. Work those and skip the others.

Key Issues for Reflection

1. Usually some other organizations do at least some of the things you do. Exactly where do you fit in the scheme of similar organizations?

2. How are important decisions made about your organization? Is that how you would like it to be in the future?

3. Reflect on the perspective and power of time in your organization.
   - How would you characterize your pace and style regarding deadlines, appointments, meeting beginnings and endings?
   - What about the overall tone: Is it deliberate, hurried, ponderous?
   - What is your style of record-keeping: Is it formal, informal, or derailed?

4. What is the importance of space in your organization? Are there important issues about the size and location of offices? Is private space or territoriality a crucial concern?

5. What are the predominant beliefs about human nature within your organization?
   • People basically look out for themselves first.
   • People tend to be hard working and committed.
   • People are a mixture of things and are variable.

6. What are the predominate beliefs about people and change?
   • People are able to change.
   • People are fixed in their behaviors.
   • Some people can change, some cannot.

7. Some organizations proceed as though nothing is impossible and any problem can be solved. Some are tentative, less sure about solving problems. What is the attitude that most prevails within your organization?

8. From your experience, what is it that most likely will keep your organization from doing what it wants to do?

9. Organizations operate differently. Here are some predominant modes. How do you see yourselves and where would you like to be?
   • It's the way we've always done it.
   • This is the right way to do it.
   • Let's refer this to the committee and do what it recommends.
   • Let's thrash it out in the committee and on the board and reach a decision.
   • Let's experiment and see if it works.
   • We need some research before we can decide what to do.

10. How would you characterize the way your last two or three executives have interacted with your board around roles, responsibilities, and decisions?

There are three more items to consider:

1. Perhaps most important, as you move to the next step in selection, is this: what are your most powerful and compelling dreams, visions and hopes for your organization? What are the strongest currents of aspiration likely to have the greatest effect on your direction?

2. In looking over your responses to the 10 questions (the key issues for reflection), where do you now feel it is most crucial for you to have a compatible view with a prospective leader? Where might differences prove to be creative and beneficial to organizational growth?

3. How set, static, and embedded in ancient culture are these descriptions of your organization? Where is the most fluidity and openness to change? In which areas does the belief "That's us, that's just the way we are" dominate?

You now have a sharper picture of your organization's personality. What does that mean for the kind of leader you select? While you probably don't want someone whose sense of organizational culture is totally the opposite of yours, you also probably don't want someone whose portrait of an organization is exactly yours. Now is the time to summarize that discussion, to clarify your sense of organizational culture.

Our Primary Organizational Challenges

Organizations that give consideration to identifying critical issues are more likely to find leadership equal to their special challenges. Here are some general questions, followed by a checklist, to help you identify the organization's current challenges.

Three Questions

- As you think about this organization in the next three years, what are the critical issues and big challenges it will face?
- As you think about the broader political environment, the economy, the issues facing the whole community, which will have the biggest impact on this organization?
- What does your sense of organization issues and broad community issues cause you to conclude about the kind of leadership you need in the next three to five years?

A Checklist

Use the following categories to help you remember special issues you may face in the next three years. Issues related to:
- funding and sources of revenue
- finance and budget management
- program development and redevelopment
- marketing and public relations
- organizational structure and inter-institutional linkage
- human resources
- facility and location

As you respond to the questions and the checklist, always ask, "So what?" What difference will all this make for this executive search and selection? What special talents must a leader have to be effective with the critical issues you now face?

The Environment in Which We Serve

Some might say that what matters most about your environment are such things as how many days of sunshine, how high the nearest mountain, and how far the sea. Perhaps, but the assessment we're addressing refers more to the economic, social, and organizational environment in your community.

You will know what aspects of your community environment are most important and most likely to have the greatest impact on your organization presently and in the near future. Think about that first, and see what you come up with and what agreement you can reach on the most impactful aspects of the broader community in which you do your work.

After that open-ended question you might wish to consider some of the following categories that we have found to have an impact on an organization's life and times.

What if anything would you say about the significance of:

- the economy
- unemployment
- local and state government
- trends in corporate and individual philanthropy
- availability of local foundations
- history of in-kind services provided
- collaborative fundraising
- parking and public transportation
- organizations doing work similar to yours
- patterns of cooperation and partnerships
- examples of full collaboration and mergers
- media attention to your sector
- any other categories you want to add

Identify all the factors of significant influence on the environment in which your organization must make its way. The inclination may be to first name those that tend to constrain your work. The trick is not to miss those that offer advantages, openings, and opportunities to expand and strengthen the particular good work that is yours to do in your own community.

Writing a Summary Statement

You may have chosen two, three, or all six ways of assessing your organization and its environment. Now is the time to pull together the notes from your board conversations. What's the sum of what you have discovered? How would you now state your present sense about your organization? In particular, how would you now answer the "tell me about your organization" question? In fact, that is probably the question you will get from someone you are hoping will refer strong candidates and from promising candidates themselves.

You may also want to gather the various impressions and notes into a coherent paragraph. When later you are called upon to produce a press release or a paragraph or two for a fact sheet or flyer used to promote the executive position, you will have it ready to go. It will also likely be more thoughtful and comprehensive having just had the self-assessment discussions.

One Final Assessment: Do We Hire an Interim Director?

This decision is not one to skip. You may very well decide that your situation is such that an interim director is not needed. Most organizations will appoint an acting director, and that may be right for your situation. Generally, an interim director is one appointed when a long search is expected or it seems like a good idea to allow some time to pass before a new, full-time executive is hired. In a fine small book, *Chief Executive Succession Planning*, Nancy Axelrod notes that "a growing number of organizations now hire interim chief executives to give the board sufficient time to determine what the organization needs in its next executive, to conduct a thorough search, or to help the organization address key issues that need attention before qualified candidates can be recruited." While we, too, experience this as an increasing trend, that is not sufficient reason for you to make that decision.

Certain factors might be in play that would strengthen the case for engaging an interim director. Some find it to be a particular important strategy when there are staffing and other issues that might usefully be addressed by the board with an interim, so that the new executive does not inherit them. Others have major initiatives or big events under way that cannot wait for the appointment of a new executive and would benefit from moving forward under the guidance of a seasoned interim director.

If you decide to engage an interim director, who do you look for and where do you find her? Our experience is the "who" includes such qualities as a mature manager who has had experience in two or more nonprofit leadership roles. That experience would have extended to strong familiarity with all aspects of nonprofit organizational life (finance, fundraising, staff management, marketing and public relations, program coordination, etc). As well, it is probably better that the prospective interim not just know management, but management in an aspect of the nonprofit sector, like your own. Geography may also play a role in the selection of a successful interim. Someone familiar with your community, or at least your part of the state, will have the advantage of not needing extended startup time to get to know the territory. In this case, the best interim candidate may be right in your organization. A seasoned staff or board member may just be the answer.

If your board does decide to go to outside your organization, here are three sources that we have found most useful in locating a good interim director candidate:

A nonprofit management support and technical assistance center. Most states have one (e.g., Ohio Association of Nonprofit Organizations and Maryland Nonprofits).

Your local community foundation. They have likely been asked the question before and with luck have developed some helpful answers.

Umbrella agencies for particular sectors of the nonprofit family of organizations. That would include local United Ways, arts councils, and organizations coordinating health and mental health systems.

For yet more detail on the who, what, and why of the interim director decision, check out the excellent article "Interim Executive Directors: The Power in the Middle" by Tim Wolfred of CompassPoint Nonprofit Services. And board presidents: don't pass up the opportunity for this conversation with your board. The right interim executive director can help greatly in keeping your organization moving forward and restoring some of the balance and stability needed during a leadership transition.

Chapter III

The Board Gets Focused: Identifying the Profile of the New Executive

Our experience is that this getting focused on the profile of a new executive includes at least four component parts: roles; abilities; personal characteristics; and experience and credentials.

- The role is specifically what you wish the executive to do.
- The abilities, skills, or competencies are the things you expect the executive to do well.
- The personal characteristics are exhibited in the leadership behavior of your executive.
- Experience and credentials, of course, are those things in the work and educational history of the candidate that you believe to be necessary in order to be able to do the job.

Two more comments before we offer suggestions on each of the components that comprise the executive profile. First, make sure that what you decide about an executive profile fits with what you concluded from your summary statement of your organizational self-assessment. Often what you conclude about your organizational situation will suggest a skill or attribute necessary to address it. Secondly, while we present distinct categories for you to work through, they are not always clearly separate one from another. For example, while the ability to write would be a skill and honesty an attribute, something like working well with people contains both natural attributes and practical skills. With that forward we go.

Roles

Board vs. Executive

Let's start with the broadest decisions about roles—those related to what you want the executive to do versus what you intend to do as a board yourself. You may have a history of doing this one way and may now have a preference for doing it another. The thing to know is that there is no single best way for all. Looking forward to a new executive and considering your present situation and its special needs, what is it you want?

Resist advice that begins "boards should always..." or "executives ought never..." There are only a few "always" and "nevers" in the world of organizational life, because there are so many special cases—special people forging working relationships in ways that work best for them. You need to decide what will be your predominant way of working as a board with the executive in your organization.

Generally speaking, boards and executives tend to operate in one of four ways. While these ways are not entirely distinct from one another, for purposes of discussion and decision about how you wish to operate, here they are in brief:

1. **Board initiates and decides, executive receives and implements.**
   This is probably the most formal way of running an organization. The board is strong, well in control, and the executive is clear about professional activity based on board directives. This tends to work well when board members are designated representatives from other organizations or control the funding sources. In this model, executives who do well are good at faithfully carrying out the decisions made by the board.

2. **Executive proposes, board disposes.**
   The executive takes the lead in developing new ideas, programs, and funding. The board critiques, amends, and decides. Board activity is focused on review and response with the executive acting as initiator. At best, a fine balance is reached between executive creativity and board control. At worst, the executive ends up lobbying ideas and the organization moves toward an adversarial mode, with innovation and creativity on one side and practicality and control on the other.

3. **Executive acts, board is informed and consulted.**
   Small organizations, or those fashioned around the abilities of a strong leader, often function in this manner. The board acts as consultant as needed, and the executive stays in the lead with the ideas and execution. If the paid leadership is consistent in consulting the board and the board is willing to have a more passive role, this can work well. If the executive fails to consult or makes decisions or takes action that embarrasses the board, it does not work well.

4. **Board and executive jointly initiate and implement.**
   This operates best where boards are willing to share power and executives are willing to share programs. Most people think that boards set policy, not executives, and that executives must design and run programs, not boards. While this mode of operation is not without merit, it does tend to keep both board and executive from being flexible enough to use the rich variety of knowledge and ability that exists in the leadership of an organization.

   For instance, most organizations have boards and executives with a mix of creativity and practicality, policy-making, and program development skills. Effective organizations find ways of using this variety of abilities without being confined by strict role definitions. However, this joint initiation and implementation process does not work well where the executive or board members, for whatever reason, want well-defined and protected roles.

There are, of course, a near-infinite number of ways to run an organization. Your own way may be a mix of the above or something quite different. The four presented are simply a starting point for discussions about partnership-building between the board and executive presently responsible for the life of the organization.

Specific Functions

Now we move from the general of what you wish your executive to do to the specifics of functions and roles within that framework. The functions we enumerate are fairly common with the life of any nonprofit organization. What we suggest is that those functions may or may not remain with the executive or the board in every aspect of organizational life. For example, you may want your executive to perform in the initiating and formulating function when it comes to marketing and public relations, but you, as a board member, want very much to be in on those functions when it comes to the broad mission and purposes of your organization.

The following organizational functions and chart may help you to think clearly about how you want your partnership to work. Begin by using a separate form for each category of the following recommended categories. (You may have others.)

- Mission and Purposes
- Program and Services
- Marketing and Public Relations
- Planning and Evaluation
- Funding and Finance
- Administration and Staffing

Second, check opposite the Leadership Function the primary party who will carry out that function. In some cases you may decide that a particular function may occur in two or more places.

Deciding Who Has the Responsibility				
Organizational function _____				
Leadership Function	Executive	Board President	Committee Chair	Board Committee	Full Board
Initiate	☐	☐	☐	☐	☐
Formulate	☐	☐	☐	☐	☐
Propose	☐	☐	☐	☐	☐
Decide	☐	☐	☐	☐	☐
Implement	☐	☐	☐	☐	☐
Monitor	☐	☐	☐	☐	☐
Evaluate	☐	☐	☐	☐	☐
Reformulate	☐	☐	☐	☐	☐

Note: In some cases more than one person or group may have the responsibility. If so, check two or more places.

Primary Executive Roles

One more way of looking at executive roles, this one borrowed from the fine research and writing of Robert Quinn. It first appeared in his book *The Master Manager*. Quinn claims that executives unavoidably are called upon to perform eight different roles. You may or may not agree with the list, but we hope it will suggest a different way of understanding and deciding upon the primary roles you want for your executive.

Mentor Role
1. Understanding self and others
2. Communicating effectively
3. Developing subordinates

Facilitator Role
1. Building teams
2. Using participative decision-making
3. Managing conflict

Monitor Role
1. Monitoring individual performance
2. Managing collective performance
3. Managing organizational performance

Coordinator Role
1. Managing projects
2. Designing work
3. Managing across functions

Director Role
1. Visioning, planning, and goal-setting
2. Designing and organizing
3. Delegating effectively

Producer Role
1. Working productively
2. Fostering a productive work environment
3. Managing time and stress

Broker Role
1. Building and maintaining a power base
2. Negotiating agreement and commitment
3. Presenting ideas

Innovator Role
1. Living with change
2. Thinking creatively
3. Creating change

Detailed Listings

Everyone seems to have his own favorite list of abilities important for executive leadership. Now it is your turn to decide upon yours. What follows are two different executive ability lists. The first set is quite detailed and based on the work of Jan Masaoka at CompassPoint and the staff at BoardSource. They offered it initially as a first draft for an executive evaluation instrument. Because of its comprehensive nature it can also be utilized as a listing of executive abilities from which you may select those most applicable and desirable for your own situation.

The second we borrowed from our own work on executive evaluation (see appendix). It focuses on nine abilities with short descriptions of each. Because of its brevity, you may find it to be more workable.

Set #1

Organization-Wide: Program Development and Delivery

a. Ensures that the organization has a long-range strategy which achieves its mission, and toward which it makes consistent and timely progress

b. Provides leadership in developing program and organizational plans with the board of directors and staff

c. Meets or exceeds program goals in quantity and quality

d. Evaluates how well goals and objectives have been met

e. Demonstrates quality of analysis and judgment in program planning, implementation, and evaluation

f. Shows creativity and initiative in creating new programs

g. Maintains and utilizes a working knowledge of significant developments and trends in the field (such as AIDS, developmental disabilities, sustainable agriculture, etc.)

Comments:

Administration and Human Resources Management

a. Divides and assigns work effectively, delegating appropriate levels of freedom and authority

b. Establishes and makes use of an effective management team

c. Maintains appropriate balance between administration and programs

d. Ensures that job descriptions are developed and that regular performance evaluations are held and documented

e. Ensures compliance with personnel policies and state and federal regulations on workplaces and employment

f. Ensures that employees are licensed and credentialed as required and that appropriate background checks are conducted

g. Recruits and retains a diverse staff

h. Ensures that policies and procedures are in place to maximize volunteer involvement

i. Encourages staff development and education, and assists program staff in relating its specialized work to the total program of the organization

j. Maintains a climate which attracts, keeps, and motivates a diverse staff of top-quality people

Comments:

Community Relations

a. Serves as an effective spokesperson for the organization; represents the programs and point of view of the organization to agencies, organizations and the general public

b. Establishes sound working relationships and cooperative arrangements with community groups and organizations

Comments:

Financial Management and Legal Compliance

a. Ensures adequate control and accounting of all funds, including developing and maintaining sound financial practices

b. Works with the staff, finance committee, and board in preparing a budget; sees that the organization operates within budget guidelines

c. Maintains official records and documents, and ensures compliance with federal, state and local regulations and reporting requirements (such as annual information returns, payroll withholding and reporting, etc.)

d. Executes legal documents appropriately

e. Assures that funds are disbursed in accordance with contract requirements and donor designations

Comments:

Fundraising

a. Develops realistic, ambitious fundraising plans

b. Meets or exceeds revenue goals, ensuring that adequate funds are available to permit the organization to carry out its work

c. Successfully involves others in fundraising

d. Establishes positive relationships with government, foundation and corporate funders

e. Establishes positive relationships with individual donors

Comments:

Relationship with Board of Directors

a. Works well with board officers

b. Provides appropriate, adequate, and timely information to the board

c. Provides support to board committees

d. Sees that the board is kept informed on the condition of the organization and all important factors influencing it

e. Works effectively with the board as a whole

Comments:

Set #2

Nine Abilities

- Conceptual Clarity/Positioning: ability to envision, articulate and place in context an idea/project

- The Product: ability to ensure its quality, its quantitative success

- Participation: ability to assist board and committee members to be significantly involved

- The Plan: ability to devise a comprehensive and feasible strategy involving appropriate board, staff and committee people

- Timeliness: ability to maintain a schedule in the execution of a plan and its final result

- Problem Management: ability to take personal responsibility, proceed positively, seek help as needed, anticipate the problems

- Linking/Connecting: ability to see and make beneficial project/people connections within and to form mutually beneficial linkages without

- Cost Control: ability to work within a budget, accommodate budgetary adjustments efficiently

- Revenue Generation: ability to identify appropriate revenue sources, develop diversity of revenue sources, establish multi-year funding sources, balance earned and unearned income

In summary, it is your task to choose those abilities for your executive profile you know to be needed. The previous two lists may assist you with that important decision.

Personal Characteristics

These you could come up with on your own, just by thinking of the kind of executive leaders you have admired. Just by thinking about the kind of people you enjoy being around, you quickly get to characteristics like honesty, integrity, non-defensiveness, sense of humor, slow to take credit and quick to give it away. With very little thought, you could add others, and should.

Perhaps what little we can add to your own natural and good insights here is to convey to you the ideas of some others whom we respect. That we will do in the form of three checklists of leader attributes that might prompt you to remember some that you failed to mention in your first response to the attributes of executive inquiry.

The first is from Peter Drucker, one of the first and best in the field of leadership and management science. The second is from the previously mentioned thoughtful research on succession from the Illinois Arts Alliance. The third is a partial list from the Guru Guide, which compiles and summarizes the best insights on leadership from a variety of leading writers and researchers.

The Drucker Executive Characteristics

We begin with Drucker.

1. Effective leaders: Ask, "What needs to be done?"

2. Ask, "What is right for the enterprise?"

3. Develop action plans.

4. Take responsibility for decisions.

5. Take responsibility for communicating.

6. Focus on opportunities rather than problems.

7. Run productive meetings.

8. Think and say "we" rather than "I."

To this listing, which is fairly comprehensive, we would add two additional characteristics: high energy and good sense of humor.

Illinois Arts Alliance Executive Characteristics

Honor the mission. The executive director must be able to embody the mission and articulate it in a way that inspires.

Focus on the big picture. Keep an eye on the horizon, make the vision a reality, and be disciplined about the big strategic plan.

Look outward, not inward. The executive is the primary figurehead for the organization to the outside world—executive as chief connector to those with whom the organization needs connection.

Be an excellent fundraiser. Others can and should help, but the executive must organize the overall plan and coordinate the efforts, as well as be the one who makes the big asks either alone or with a key board colleague.

Be multidimensional. The executive must know about and, now and again, touch all aspects of the organization. As noted in the report, "It's a little like a spider in the middle of a web."

Work well with people. With staff and board and sometimes volunteers, the executive is the chief people person connecting, inspiring, engaging the key individuals without, as well as within, the organization.

Accept low pay and long hours. The executive is best who thrives on intrinsic rewards and has high energy. Those who feel easily victimized by either and given to whining will not likely do well.

Guru Guide Leadership and Management Characteristics

Most executives need to involve themselves in practices related to management and those related to leadership. We believe, for the chief staff person, it is the leadership characteristics that are primary and must prevail. Here are 10 for your consideration:

Innovator
Planner
Focuses on people
Relies on trust
Aligns people with a direction
Emphasizes philosophy, values, and goals
Has long-term focus
Asks what and why
Seeks change
Inspires others to follow

These are some attributes for review as you build your own list. The attributes you decide upon should be added to your list of abilities and roles to form the major portion of your executive profile. But now on to the final component: experience and credentials.

Experience and Credentials

Experience

Most boards want to select executives who have experience. The question is what does that mean? How much is enough? What specific kind of experience is expected? This category is mostly in the realm of your own organizational preference. For that reason we give you a list of questions for your discussion so you can conclude what length and type of experience you want.

- Is there a difference between how much experience is required vs. desired?
- In what kind of work settings will the ideal candidate have experience?
- In what kind of role, at what level, and with what title was this work experience?
- What experiences are absolutely key to our executive role?
- What are the must-ask questions about the candidate's experience?
- What will best demonstrate the desired level of depth of experience more than mere words?
- For what lack of experience should we be on alert?
- What for us is the relationship between the number of years of experience and its quality and diversity?

Credentials

As a guide and comparison, consider that the overwhelming majority of nonprofit executives in all sizes of organizations have four-year bachelor degrees. Depending on the size of the organization, about 20% to 66% have master's degrees of one kind or another. It is up to you to determine how important graduate study is and how it ranks with depth of experience.

There are four major questions about credentials you may wish to consider and ask:

- What is the preferred educational background for this candidate?
- What kind of degrees do you prefer?
- What level of degree do you prefer?
- Which accreditations or certifications do you require?

Compiling an Executive Profile

By now, with your notes and board discussions on the executive profile, you may have more than enough on roles, abilities, personal characteristics, and experiences and credentials. This is the time for you to get it down to a summary page for ease of communication with your search committee. The search committee will, no doubt, do a yet smaller version for press releases, referral sources, flyers, and the candidates themselves. In the course of this editing and shrinking exercise it will be helpful to think about priorities. The perfect candidate who fits all your requirements may not appear. While surely you do not want too much lowering of standards and expectations, neither do you want requirements that are too high, too rigid, and that therefore lead to disappointment.

Try this. List for yourselves the top three to five criteria from your discussions about roles, abilities, attributes, and experiences (including credentials). That should result in a fairly good summary of an executive profile.

You may wish to put this list in the form of a narrative. Whatever you decide, what you are aiming for here is focus. The other important word here is discipline. From this point forward you will need the discipline to stay on track and faithful to the organizational self-assessment and executive profile on which you have spent so much time and to which you have given so much thought.

Perhaps the biggest mistake made in executive search is forgetting about or setting aside those carefully considered guides and getting lost in résumés and interviews. Bring the summaries along with you throughout the process. Post them up at every board and search committee meeting if you must. Carry forward this very thoughtful work, and your chances of a successful and satisfying outcome will be very high.

A Word About Position Descriptions

As a board, you could decide that since you have defined the role, abilities, characteristics, and credentials, you will ask the search committee to outline a position description for your executive. If you do choose to do so, you should review and approve it. In either case, it does need to get done either at this point or as one of the first items of business of the search committee.

We pass along three thoughts about the position description that we have found to be useful. First, and most important, it should flow from and match with the essence of the summary statements mentioned in the previous chapter. Write your position description based upon the clarifying and focusing work done on the organizational self-assessment and the executive profile. With these two documents you have built a solid foundation for the search. Now is the time to make use of it.

Secondly, locate the previous position description utilized for the executive who is departing. There are two good reasons for this, and one bad one. The bad one would be the temptation to copy it and just forget about all the good new work you have done. On the positive side it may prompt you to remember something which you have left out of the new description. Most importantly, by comparing new and old, you will see the changes, the new emphasis, additions, and fresh ways of talking about the position. That will keep you focused on the kind of person you want now, rather than what may have been appropriate for a day gone by.

Finally, you will need a long form (up to two pages) and a short form (summary paragraph) of the position description. The longer form will be of particular value in interview conversations with candidates. The shorter form will be the one most valuable as you utilize various communication strategies to create your pool of candidates. On both forms make sure that you include an all inclusive equal opportunity statement. For your review, we have included two sample position descriptions in Appendix I.

Decisions About Internal Candidates

This issue can be difficult and in fact may create difficulty. You should keep in mind three important points as you work your way through the decision regarding an internal candidate.

First, communicate clearly to the staff and the rest of the board that you will be accepting applications from internal candidates, if that is the case. If it is not, communicate with equal clarity that you have determined that, for this next executive, you want to select a candidate from outside the organization.

Secondly, take care to deal with any inside candidate with special care and confidentiality if you choose to receive such candidate. The internal candidate is in the sensitive and difficult position of continuing to do his or her work, while competing for the job. If it is a board member, it is best that she take a leave of absence during the period of the search.

Finally, the committee should keep the executive profile firmly in mind as it considers all candidates, but especially the one on the inside. It may be tempting to shorten the process and sidestep the tough work of the search by moving quickly to hire a fairly strong internal candidate. If such a candidate is to prevail in the search it must be on the grounds of clear comparison, not only to the profile and position description, but also to a field of candidates that emerges from the careful creation of a broad and talented candidate pool.

Chapter IV

The Search Committee:
Selection and Initial Tasks

In this section we will focus on two important issues: the work the board must do in creating a balanced, diverse, and representative search committee, and the initial focus of the work for that search committee. In creating a search committee, the board needs to address three important questions: who will be on the committee, what will be the size of the committee, and who will do the staffing for the committee work.

The search committee begins its own work by addressing four issues: what is the board saying about the state of our organization and the preferred executive profile; what are the details of the board and guidelines for our work; how will we go about creating a high-quality pool of candidates; and what do we do about internal and external communication during the course of the search.

Search Committee Selection

The board's work of selecting the search committee needs to address the issues of size, representation, and staffing. These three important issues are addressed in what follows.

Size

Although you may be involving or consulting with a large number of people along the way, perhaps it is best that the committee itself be kept small and workable. We could imagine smaller organizations having only six members and larger organizations with multiple political sensitivities expanding to nine. The downside of either are obvious: lack of broad enough representation on the one hand, or difficulty moving the process forward with timely decision-making on the other.

Representation and Membership Qualities

The list of categories of people who should be considered for membership on the search committee is a fairly extensive one. It would include: the board president, previous board members, present board members, staff, volunteers/committee members, community leaders, clients, current executive director, and interim director. The key word here is "considered," because, depending on your particular situation, some of these probably should not be search committee members, but should be in the category of those to consult.

For ease of consideration, and to assist you through this critical task of establishing a balanced, diverse, and representative search committee, we have created this chart which represents our best thinking based on a fairly large variety of executive searches. As you go through this, do keep in mind that, while representation is of great importance, you need also consider skills and personal characteristics of potential members of the search committee. That's next.

Deciding on Search Committee Representation			
Category	**Advisability**	**Comment**	**Number**
Board President	Probably Not	Must attend to running the organization	—
Previous Board Members	Yes	Experience, history, demonstrated loyalty	1–2
Present Board Members	Yes	Ongoing and future leadership; knowledge of organizational assessment and executive profile	2–3
Staff	Probably Not	Knows operational issues; questions of confidentiality and favoritism	0
Volunteer/Committee Members	Probably	Next group of new board members; history of dependable work	1–2
Important Community Constituents	Probably	Outsider view; question of time and commitment	1
Clients	Probably Not	First-hand experience of work; question of lacking organizational experience	0
Interim Director	Maybe	Experience; question of time away from organizational work	1
Current/Just Departed Executive	Probably Not	Making a clean break and facing forward	—
TOTAL			6–9

You will notice that we have never said "never." Some experts we know, and some writers we have read, do clearly say "no" to including certain potential categories of people on the search committee. We may mostly agree with the recommendation not to involve the present executive and present board president, but we can imagine some circumstances, related to a very small organization or where an executive departs for health reasons, that flexibility and generosity of spirit may prevail over what should ordinarily be the case. You will know. We believe that if your judgments are carefully considered, then these judgments will be right for your selection.

There are other qualities to consider beyond mere representation that make for an effective search committee. Most of them would come to your mind as you consider appointments to the committee. But here are a few to jog your memory—a few for you to consider as you decide on search committee membership.

- **Confidentiality.** It is important that committee deliberations be candid and clear with no need to worry about confidentiality.

- **Commitment.** The work of the committee will take no small amount of time. People appointed must be trusted to make this a priority.

- **Decision-Making Skill.** You do not want people who rush decisions or those who are given to lengthy procrastination and indecision.

- **Direct Communication.** You want people who will speak their minds clearly and directly so you do not have to guess what they are feeling or thinking.

- **Non-Defensive.** You do not want to spend large amounts of time taking care of people's feelings. Overly argumentative and defensive people can greatly slow the process.

Finally, you will want to keep in mind diversity of gender, race, and age. Perhaps somewhat less obvious are diversity of occupation and length of significant involvement with the organization. For example, having too many attorneys is probably not a good idea and will tend to limit the perspective of the committee. Likewise, a search committee membership made up only of people with 10 or more years' experience with your organization may be less than desirable. A mix of those who know the history and those who are unaware of "what we tried" and "what doesn't work" is usually a good thing.

Committee Staffing

Ordinarily the chair of the search committee will be appointed by the board president. The board president will have in mind such qualities as a sense of organizational history and ability to conduct effective meetings. Strongly consider having a support or administrative person, whether this role is filled by an internal staff member or someone external to the organization. There will be notes to be taken, meetings to be set, and communications that must happen on schedule. For a member of the committee to do that work is, of course, possible, but it then does limit his ability to participate. Sometimes we have seen a previous board member fill the staffing role (not as a member of the committee). Other organizations have utilized a trusted, retired volunteer to assist with the administrative tasks of the committee. The key is someone who is organized, tends to detail, and can be trusted to be confidential.

Now, with the search committee in place, the initial, foundational work of the board is done. We turn our attention to the first work of the search committee.

Search Committee: First Work

The very first work of the search committee can be outlined in four steps: understanding the board's organizational assessment and executive profile; clarifying the board's guidelines for the search; creating a pool of candidates; and initiating a communication plan. The most important considerations in each of those steps are addressed in what follows.

Understanding the Board's Organizational Assessment and Executive Profile

The very first work of the search committee (other than checking in to make sure you all know one another) is to fully understand the clarity and focus that the board attained in its organizational self-assessment and preparation of the executive profile. It should help that two or three current board members have gone through that clarifying and focusing experience. The good news is that this is substantial foundational work that you, as a search committee, need not do. Your job is to fully understand and faithfully carry forward this clarity and focus throughout the search process.

For sure that means, at least, what is contained in the summary assessment noted at the end of Chapter III. It very well may mean getting further into the board's thinking by gaining access to the notes and reflections from each section of the organizational assessment and the executive profile. Now is the time to clarify anything which is not clear and to challenge (if need be) anything you may question. But since the board is finally responsible for the search and selection, it is its intention and guidance that ultimately needs to be honored.

Clarifying the Board's Guidelines

The board, through its members on your committee, can convey the results of its deliberations on organizational assessment and executive profile. If any important guidelines have not been decided by the board, there may be a need for a joint meeting of the board and search committee to reach agreement on those issues. If that seems like too many voices in one room, the board may wish to ask its executive committee to meet with the search committee. Either way, the board and search committee need to have a full discussion and reach a friendly, full agreement.

What follows are five not-so-small details crucial to the work of the search committee: preferred timeline; completion of the committee's work; salary and benefit package; committee budget; and number of candidates to recommend to the board. A word about each.

The Preferred Timeline

We say preferred because there does need to be a preference, a goal that all believe is not only preferable but doable. This should not be an "if everything goes perfectly" kind of timeline, but one that allows for some amount of extra time to accommodate the dreaded, though likely, unexpected. You may also, at this time, wish to agree upon a plan B timeline, which covers major interruptions and problems such as candidates backing out.

You will note, perhaps remember, the sample timeline worth discussing with your board in Chapter I under "It Will Take Time and Resources" (p. 4). You very well may ask to adjust it to fit your situation, but it is, at least, a starting point for the conversation.

Completion of the Committee's Work

This one is seemingly obvious but not necessarily so. For some, the work of the committee is over when the favored candidate is presented and a contract signed. For others, the board asks the committee to stay active for the symbolic first 100 days of the new executive's tenure to assist with getting off to a good start. That would include some of the items to be addressed in Chapter VII, such as orientation, introduction to key people within and without the organization, goal-setting, and deciding upon an evaluation procedure.

In the best situation, the individual search committee members were fully informed about this matter when they were recruited. If not, the answer to the "when is our work completed" question needs to be clarified at this point.

Salary Range and Benefit Package

While the details of the final offer to the candidate are addressed in Chapter V, now is the time for an early estimate and guideline for what that would look like. There are usually more items to discuss and decide upon than most boards and search committees imagine. In order to be as comprehensive as possible, we have included a checklist for your review. The answer to some of the items may be "not to be included," but at least you will have the advantage early on of considering all the possible salary and benefit questions to be addressed.

Compensation and Benefit Items for Consideration

- Base salary or draw
- Sign-on bonus
- Annual or performance bonuses (eligibility/range/when paid)
- Commissions
- Relocation package
- Health insurance
- Dental insurance
- Vision provision
- Prescription provision
- Disability
- Life insurance
- Cafeteria/flexible benefits options
- Pension and retirement plan 401k
- Vehicle allowance
- Professional development
- Educational assistance
- License fees
- Personal leave
- Sick leave
- Vacation/holiday
- Computer
- Parking
- Membership in associations, clubs
- Journal subscriptions

Committee Budget

It does cost money to conduct a search. Usually, the largest expenses are incurred in the hiring of a search firm or an individual consultant. It is our intention that those expenses will not be necessary for most small to medium-large organizations with budgets ranging from $100,000 to $1 million. With this small book and an active board and search committee, most searches should cost in the range of $2,500 to $7,500. In Chapter I (p. 5) two sample budgets were outlined. Now would be the time to review those budgets and match them with the expenses you anticipate. The search committee needs to know from the board, at this early place in its work, just what kind of expenses it can accrue and organize its work around that reality.

Number of Candidates to Recommend to the Board

The primary question here to clarify is whether the committee brings to the board one final candidate or more than one. There is some difference of opinion on this matter. We would recommend, in most cases, to bring one finalist to the table as the committee's best conclusion to the executive search. Oftentimes, the committee will bring in their rating of the next two to four with an analysis or explanation.

The board may decide to allow final candidates to meet members of the staff. While that seems like a generous and inclusive gesture, that very gesture may cause some staff members to assume that they have a vote or, worse, veto power. This decision should be kept in the hands of the board.

The board, after meeting the finalist, does, of course, have the right to reject the committee's number one candidate and ask to meet another finalist. If that seems necessary this all must happen quickly and confidentially, so as not to lose a candidate or jeopardize her own need to be confidential.

Now armed with a clear understanding of the board's organizational assessment, executive profile, and guidelines for the conduct of the search, we turn to the very public matter of creating a pool of high-quality candidates.

Creating a Pool of Candidates

The short and strong message here is, "You need to have a lot of good people to choose from." If the pool is small, if the quality is mediocre, a top-notch candidate will not magically appear. Another short and almost as strong message is, "The candidate for whom you are looking may very well not be looking." There is nothing wrong with taking a hard look at candidates who are looking to move. There is everything right about finding and approaching strong candidates who were not planning to move.

Beyond these opening edicts, we will work with you in this section on three matters that will assist you in creating a high quality pool of candidates. In order, they are: the value of diversity; identifying potential applicants; and information and instruction for the candidates.

The Value of Diversity

No doubt, some of the direction on this one has come through, in written and verbal communications, from your board. We say consider the issues of gender, race, and age. "Consider" means having an open and honest discussion in the committee. This does not refer to what the law requires (although that is worth discussing); rather, this is about your own particular mix of values and organizational requirements. What is it that you care about in this matter? What do you want to make sure gets communicated about your organization throughout this process? If, in fact, you conclude that diversity is a strong value for you, achieving a diverse pool of candidates will not happen by accident. It requires a commitment to make diversity a priority and a recruitment plan that targets people and places that will ensure a diverse mix of candidates. Our own view is that this is a good thing that goes far beyond a "p.r. thing" or a "p.c. thing." It puts your organization in a position to find and attract strong candidates that too many others do not work at finding and, perhaps, even do not care to do the work of attracting.

Identifying Potential Applicants

The first step here is to get the very best ideas of the committee (and ask the board as well). It could be that you already know the contact person or organization that will get you the very best candidate. It even could be that someone among you already knows the best candidate. To get at this obvious and often most productive first step in creating a pool of candidates, try these questions and contact points.

- Do we already know someone who could be a strong candidate?

- Who are the people in our sector who can help us find ideal candidates?

- Who are the top leaders, the key players in your sector?

- Was there someone we interviewed for this or another senior position that we should now consider?

- Is there someone from another sector who has broad enough interests and experiences for us to contact?

- Is there a present volunteer, or past or present board member, that we should not overlook?

- What organizations in our sector are most respected, and is there someone there that we should consider?

Two additional contact points are colleges and professional associations.

Colleges:
- What schools graduate candidates with the skills that we need?

- Do we have any classmates that we should look up?

- Is there any way to take a look at the alumni list for people in our sector?

- Are there any professors or staff members that could help in our search?

Professional Associations:

- What professional associations do we belong to?

- What other associations should we target for this search?

- Are there any outstanding members we could recommend to help on the search?

- Are there any members we should target as candidates?

- Is there a way we could network directly with this group?

- Is there a way we could get the membership list?

More Good Sources for Good Candidates

In general, getting the word out and finding high-quality candidates is first and best done by the kind of direct, personal contact suggested above. Working this network should be a first priority. It is not the only place, merely the first. You may want to place advertisements on web sites and mailing lists, newspapers and journals. Following are some that can get you started.

- Nonprofit web sites
  - ☐ Guidestar.org
  - ☐ Asaenet.org

- Networking web sites
  - ☐ Linkedin.com
  - ☐ Ziggs.com
  - ☐ Spoke.com
  - ☐ Xing.com

- General information web sites
  - ☐ Wikipedia.com
  - ☐ Superpages.com

- Search engines
  - ☐ Google.com
  - ☐ Alive.com
  - ☐ Yahoo.com
  - ☐ Alfaseek.com
  - ☐ Jux2.com
  - ☐ Exalead.com

- Publications
  - ☐ The Nonprofit Quarterly
  - ☐ The Chronicle of Philanthropy
  - ☐ The Chronicle of Higher Education
  - ☐ Local business journals in adjacent states
  - ☐ City and state magazines

- Other Organizations
  - ☐ Junior League
  - ☐ United Way
  - ☐ Chamber of Commerce
  - ☐ National Society of Fund Raising Executives
  - ☐ American Society of Association Executives
  - ☐ Volunteer organizations
  - ☐ Organizations of marketing professionals
  - ☐ Professional fraternities and sororities

- Other Resources
  - ☐ School web sites/professors/career services
  - ☐ Alumni web sites of regional colleges and universities
  - ☐ Company web sites
  - ☐ Job posting web sites
  - ☐ Résumé web sites
  - ☐ Membership directories
  - ☐ Outplacement web sites
  - ☐ Web sites that target diverse audiences

All of the above are not of equal value, and all options are not mentioned above. This aspect of creating a pool of candidates requires your own best ingenuity related to your town, city and state.

Information and Instructions for the Candidates

In terms of information, all prospective candidates or those requesting it should at least receive:

- The short position description
- A profile of your organization
- A brief outline of the timeline and process of the search
- Contact information for the chair of the search committee or someone appointed to fill the role of contact with the candidates

Candidates should also receive clear instructions about what is asked of them. For example:

- Completion of your application form
- Questions to be addressed in a letter
- Résumé
- References
- Their desires about confidentiality

Finally, of course, you must decide how much to communicate at this stage and exactly what it is you wish to ask of the candidates.

Designing the Communication Plan

Perhaps the first thing to say is that all communication around the search, whether to staff, board, volunteers, candidates, key stakeholders outside, or the general public through press releases, should be brief, timely, and clear. It should also have a tone that contains the kind of truth that neither overstates nor oversells, understates nor undersells the position or the status of the organization.

There are four main points in the search process of particular importance in a communication plan. The first centers around the departure of your executive. The departing executive should have the opportunity to do this first to all internal colleagues and to key external stakeholders by personal letter before the organizational press release is issued.

The second point is the announcement of the search. That announcement should contain the abbreviated form of the executive profile, the names of those whom the board has appointed to the search committee, and the timeline, together with the contact person, which is usually the chair of the search committee. Again, after informing all those internal to the organization, a letter can be sent to key stakeholders before issuing a press release.

The third period is that in-between time. The board should be informed regularly and at least via a verbal report to the chair every two weeks. A slightly more formal written report should be forwarded once a month to the board. This is a crucial, priority matter. Since the search committee was formed by the board and finally submits the results of its work to the board, the committee should faithfully report on its progress and answer any and all concerns when the board may have them.

To keep staff informed, the search committee chair might choose to appear monthly at a staff meeting so they feel in the know about this important process. Any concerns or questions that arise from the staff should be responded to in a timely and open fashion without betraying any confidentiality that pertains to particular candidates. The staff should ideally feel no undue secrecy or exclusion from this process, so important to the life of the whole organization.

For key stakeholders, one or two written updates on the progress of the search is sufficient. Once again, if anyone within this group has questions or concerns, they can and should be dealt with on a personal and confidential basis.

Finally, and happily, comes the announcement of the new executive—first to staff and volunteers, then to stakeholders by letter containing an abbreviated biography, and lastly, in a press release with the same information. In this case, the board is in the lead on the first announcement communication. The new executive can follow with a personal letter to internal people and stakeholders with a "glad to be here and looking forward to working with you" tone.

A final comment on communications around the search. As with so many other things in life, what really gets communicated is far more than words on paper or the words that come from your mouth. The strongest, clearest messages about the search and your organization get communicated in action and behavior. A search is, after all, one of the most public and far- reaching activities of your organization. The question is what really are the organizational messages you wish to convey. Our guess is those messages have to do with words like *open* and *transparent* rather than *secretive* and *defensive*; *humane* and *thoughtful* rather than *coldly efficient*, *organized*, and *effective* rather than *unclear, unsure,* and *in disarray.*

It might not be a bad idea to review now and again those organizational messages you are sending out that go beyond the language you speak, and the words you write.

Before going forward into the exciting work of application reviews and interviews, here are a few things to "don't forget."

Don't Forget

1. **Enjoy the process.** You will meet new people, have new insights about your organization and have the satisfaction that you have done a very important piece of work for your organization.

2. **Take time.** Going without an executive is uncomfortable; going with the wrong one is disastrous. Also, a slower pace is likely to bring more rewards to everyone.

3. **Say "no" promptly and thoughtfully.** The inescapable fact is that you will disappoint 20 to 100 candidates and make one happy. If they hear quickly and with a note of thanks, they too will be speaking good words about your organization.

4. **Don't overcompensate.** Sometimes boards have a tendency to select an executive who is either the same as or the opposite of the previous one. This is probably not wise. Stay focused on the profile and your organizational assessment.

5. **Keep moving and keep top candidates informed.** *Deliberate* speed but also deliberate *speed*. And don't lose a candidate you are really interested in by not keeping him informed of the timing of the process.

6. **Remember that an executive search is also organizational promotion.** The process, the materials, the quality of the communication all present an image of your organization. You want it, of course, to be a high-quality one.

Chapter V
The Search Committee: Applications and Interviews

Getting to know the candidates on paper and in person just may be the most exciting and challenging aspect of your executive search—presuming you have been able to create a pool of candidates with 50 to 100 or more applicants as you had hoped. After reading and sorting, that number would typically be whittled down to 10 or 12. Telephone interviews would probably eliminate half of those or more. You would then have face-to-face interviews with the candidates that would result in two or three highly regarded people that would come back for a second interview. This step would lead to the selection of your preferred candidate to recommend to the board.

It is this process, which we have collapsed into one paragraph, that will no doubt take you eight to 10 weeks, and no small amount of exciting discoveries, strong conversations, and personal satisfaction. You really should count on it, look forward to it, and, with the assistance of the paragraphs that follow, make your way through it in a thoughtful and organized fashion.

We will begin with the application, and some notes about what the application means for your process. We also offer some samples of alternatives, and a few hints about reading and rating.

We will then address the first round of interviews, which includes telephone and in-person conversations, and questions, format, and rating ideas for each.

Finally, we will address the second and final round of interviews; more questions to utilize; some ideas about hospitality and introductions; and rating and selecting a finalist to present to your board.

The Application

For many people an application means a form to fill out. It could be. It also might be five questions on a page or three questions in a letter. We will, in what follows, explore those alternatives as well as a way for you to read and rate what you get back.

Designing an Application

The key question is, "What do you want to know before deciding to meet this candidate?" Our experience is that some of that will be on résumés, but some will not. Since you do want to end up with comparable information, you may want to design a simple application to accompany the résumé.

One suggestion is to develop an application with three sections:

a. Use the executive profile you developed with Chapter III. Ask applicants to check the qualities they believe most represent their own leader strengths, as well as those they are yet developing or perfecting. You will then be able to relate these responses to your list of most important. You will also discover the level of the applicants' self understanding and her willingness to note areas requiring development.

b. Select two or three of the organizational issues from your work with Chapter II. Choose the ones that caused the liveliest discussion for your board. Ask for a paragraph or two from the applicant about how he views this aspect of an organization. What is the applicant's view of the kind of organizational culture he is most comfortable in and used to working with?

These two questions to the candidates have the advantage of focusing this first step in the screening process directly on your core work with organizational assessment and executive profile.

c. Ask the applicant to describe which aspects of the résumé she feels are most important to your executive position.

Note: This approach is likely to weed out the great mass of résumé senders who have no particular interest in your organization. It also will probably introduce you to some interesting people who have taken the time to respond and thereby have produced for you some comparable information.

This particular idea for an application can be implemented on a one-page form, which allows about one paragraph for each of the three questions. Being on one page, it forces the candidate to be brief and focused, enabling the committee to read less and know more.

A second idea would be to ask four or five shorter questions, again on a one-page form for ease of reading and discipline of writing. Some of the early, "getting to know you" kinds of questions that we have found most productive include:

- How would you describe yourself as a person?

- What career goals do you have for yourself?

- Why have you chosen a career in nonprofit work?

- As you read the position description, about which items do you feel most and least comfortable?

- As you read the summary of our organization assessment, what intrigues you? What challenges do you see?

- What do you believe to be the chief differences between the executive practices and behaviors where you now work versus our situation?

- In what way does the timing of the availability of our position fit with your own life and the life of your present organization?

- In what way does our position fit with your career plan?

- What do you believe to be the most significant issues and trends in nonprofit leadership and governance?

- Most people differentiate between a job, a career and life's work. How would you describe your life's work?

So there are 10 questions to get you started. Choose any four or five for your own application or add others. The one-page format and short answers will prove to be beneficial.

Yet one more idea. Ask for a one-page letter to accompany the résumé. In it, you would ask the candidate to do two things: 1) tell us what it is that you would like us to know about you; and, 2) respond to the position description with comments about where you seem like the perfect candidate and where you would need to grow.

With this approach, you get at least three things: what kinds of things the candidate selects by way of self-introduction and what he chooses to leave out; how willing the candidate is to be open about his own learning and growth challenges; and writing ability, since this method will in effect call for a short essay.

Rating the Applications

A word of advice for search committee chairs: Keep it simple. Since your committee will be reviewing many applications, you need a short and fair way to begin your screening conversations. Perhaps you may wish to devise a short, half-page form that would look like this:

Name of Applicant: _____

Response	Rating (circle)	Comments (required)	Phone interview? (y or n)
1	5 4 3 2 1	_____	_____
2	5 4 3 2 1	_____	_____
3	5 4 3 2 1	_____	_____
Etc.	5 4 3 2 1	_____	_____

Name of Reader: _____

You must decide if you want all committee members to read all 50 to 100 applications. An alternative would be that one or two people would scan all for their competencies and appropriateness (you could easily eliminate 20%), then the whole committee reads those that remain. Yet another alternative is to have two or three committee members each read a third or a fourth of the applications. Depending on the total number received and the comfort level the committee has with one another, you may choose one or another alternative. In any case, the goal here is to get down to 10 or 12 with whom you are willing to have telephone conversations.

The key steps addressed in this section are the telephone interview, questions for the face-to-face interview, and comments about what the format and rating for each will be. We would, at this point, add a brief word about scheduling since it will be no small matter for multiple candidates and multiple interviewers. This is one of those points where having staff assistance would be a great advantage. But, whether or not you have that help, do not forget to calculate into your timeline that telephone interviews require at least a week's advance notice, and in-person interviews as much as two to three weeks, if travel is involved.

Telephone Screening

This may be a new experience for some or most members of the committee. Here are some considerations, which will increase the chance that it goes well.

- Remember that no matter how many people are present during the interview, the candidate needs to know who is in the room whether they speak or not.

- A speaker phone is a must.

- Decide if all or part of the committee will sit in on each conversation.

- One option is that, while all are present, only two or three participate in asking the lead questions.

- Have five or six major questions and ask the same ones of all candidates.

- Ask the applicant to send her salary history at this point in the process.

- 20 to 30 minutes will likely be enough.

- The call should end with thanks and a review of next steps.

Certain responses on the application form may intrigue you, or may even cause concern or elicit further questions. If you have six major questions for the phone interview, our guess is that three or four will have grown out of this written information sent by the candidate. These are the "I noticed you wrote…" or "Can you say something more about…" questions. They may also be, "In your application response you didn't say anything about…" or "What would you say today…" Or they may be, "I didn't fully understand what you meant by…" or "Could you give me some more on…" You may then wish to ask an additional two or three questions from those not utilized in the sample application questions on pages 41 and 42. Remember that good follow-up questions are often the most productive, so be sure to allow time for them.

A note about rating and ranking at this step in the selection: Consider allowing at least 15 minutes between telephone interviews for discussion and preliminary decisions, and then 30 minutes at the end, to decide what four to six candidates you would like to invite for personal interviews. You may not need a rating sheet. Simple notes on your reactions may be enough. Allow for more than a yes or no rating, with an unsure indicating that you need other impressions before deciding.

A reminder about prompt notification. As soon as you have selected those for telephone interviews, the other applicants not included should be thanked and told that, this time, they have not been selected as semi-finalists. A letter signed by the chair or the search committee would help engender positive regard for your organization. Likewise, those who participated in telephone interviews but not selected for personal interviews should receive a prompt, personalized letter from the committee chair.

In-Person Interviews

At this point, you are getting close. You now should have four to six strong candidates from whom you will select two or three for a second interview on a different day, one to two weeks later. People do look, sound, and act differently depending on the day, and that is a strong argument against single interviews. You now have the history and notes from the application ratings and the telephone interview. Point one is that you want to make sure that this in-person interview not only builds upon this previous information, but greatly broadens and deepens your understanding of the candidate.

As the telephone screening questions related to some application responses, so should the interview questions relate to things you heard or didn't hear in the telephone conversation. Continue to use the device of followup—"you said on the telephone… say more" or "I didn't fully understand…" or "you didn't say anything about…" This kind of question that builds on the last conversation and focuses upon yet more and deeper understanding will likely get you more of what you need to make a good decision.

Beyond that, here is yet an additional approach, which may be useful to you. In line with the discipline of staying connected and grounded in the initial organizational assessment and position description, try the following two categories of questions. First, refer to the summary of the organizational assessment and then ask:

- What is your reaction to what is contained in this organizational self-assessment?

- What, in your own executive experience, relates to the challenges implied in the assessment?

- What further questions might you have of an organization that spoke this way about itself?

Secondly, the candidate in the application and, perhaps, in the telephone interview has had the opportunity to react to the position description as it pertains to him. Probe a bit further with such questions as:

- Where you felt very comfortable relative to an item in the position description, give us an example of how that strength was exemplified in your own present organization.

- Where you mentioned a need to learn or grow give us more specifics. What would that be and how would you imagine you could attain that learning and growth?

- Is there something left out of the position description or included in it that surprises you? Why? What would you add knowing now a bit more about our organization?

One additional category of questions that might be appropriate at this point would explore the hopes and vision that the candidate might have for your organization.

- Insofar as you know us as an organization, what are some things you could envision for us in the future?

- When and how would you start working on that vision, if you were selected as our executive?

- What would you see as the role of the board in the visioning process, if you were our executive?

The ranking and rating question must be asked yet again in the context of the in-person interview. Perhaps the first thing to say is that the whole committee should be included at this important juncture. What that requires is that there needs to be a plan, in advance, as to who asks the lead questions. Of course, any and all members may chime in with a follow-up question. Once again, ample time should be allotted between interviews for full discussion and preliminary rating as to whether the particular candidate should be invited back for a second interview. You may choose to utilize a simple rating sheet or personal notes or impressions. The important thing is to share assessments immediately upon completion of the interview and to allow enough time for all reactions.

The goal here is to get down to two or three candidates for second interviews. If you have built this step around the application and telephone interview process, if you have as well broadened and deepened your understanding of the candidates with further questions and concrete examples, you will no doubt be prepared to select the finalists. This is all very systematic and intentional, and that is a good thing. You should also be relaxed enough to answer perhaps the most important question: Do I like this person well enough to want them in my life and the life of my organization for the next five to nine years?

For search committee chairs—a final checklist for this first round of interviews:

- Schedule comfortably in advance.

- Agree upon a rating system.

- Decide whether all or part of the committee will rate all applications and participate in all telephone interviews.

- Be clear about who will ask the key questions.

- Be sure all present know they are expected to ask good follow-up questions.

- Refrain from speeches and too much talk. The ratio should be at least 80 to 20 in favor of the candidate.

- Send prompt and personal letters to those not being considered further.

- Do not dismiss any of the four to six semi-finalists until the position is offered and accepted.

- Remember to keep your focus on the organizational assessment and the executive profile.

- Remember (and remind committee members) also to stay relaxed and in touch with whether you actually like this candidate.

And now, forward to the final interviews and the finalists to be selected for presentation to the board.

The Interview: The Finalists Return

This time around, and at this step in the process, the interview remains important, but of nearly equal importance is the organizational information you will want to convey and the introductions and connections you will want to make. To put it in another way, the previous interviews were organized around the committee asking and the candidate talking. This final interview will necessitate the committee doing more talking, even selling the organization and the city. There will be more dialogue, less monologue, more a mix of asking and telling on the part of both parties. You will be moving toward deciding on a favored candidate to be presented to the board.

More Questions, More Information

Prior to the second interview with the finalists, send off to them some basic documents, such basics as: your most recent IRS Form 990; the past and present year budgets; major sources of income; board names, affiliations, and terms; mission statement and outline of program areas; organizational chart; flyers or printed promotional materials; and recent news clippings. No doubt the web site has been already checked out. Perhaps some of the above documents have been passed out at a previous stage in the process. Maybe there are other materials you have that the candidates should know about. Most search committees at this point also pass along information on their city and region—the vacation and visitors' bureau kind of things, together with economic, employment, and other demographic data about the area.

A good place to start the interview is by asking the candidates if they have any questions or observations that came from reviewing the documents sent. You will gain yet another perspective on the candidates from what it is they choose to focus on and ask questions about. Having few or no observations, questions, or concerns around the packet of materials will communicate one kind of message. Having lots of anxious questions about lots of different things will communicate another. Coming prepared with a manageable number of thoughtful questions will have yet another effect. Some of the most valuable "interviewing" is going on in these final exchanges.

There yet remain some final, wrap-up kinds of questions that can be useful at this point. These could occur after having interacted with the candidate over her responses to the materials sent. Here are a few for your consideration:

- How would you evaluate, and what would you change about, this search process to date?

- What are the chief reservations you have with this position?

- Do you have any personal, family, or lifestyle reservations relative to this position?

- In what way is the position and our organization different from how you perceived it in the beginning?

- Have you experienced anything in your interactions with us or your reading of the materials that would make you want to make changes in our organization?

- If you were given this position, how would you begin your work with us? What would you want to do in the first 100 days?

- In what way, if at all, would you tend to utilize our previous executive director?

- In what way do you perceive that the culture of our organization is different from the one in which you now serve? Based on your experience, what adjustments or changes would you move toward making?

- What have been your experiences with cooperation and collaboration with other organizations? To the extent that you believe they should be explored, with what local organizations would you want to begin that exploration?

- What is there about our organization, or this position, that makes you most enthusiastic about being our executive director?

Hospitality and Introductions

These final conversations with your best candidates are always a careful, sometimes curious, mixture of listening and assessing on the one hand and speaking and selling on the other. Early on, with lots of candidates and little information about any of them, you were in the listening and assessing mode and they were predominantly speaking and selling. Now, the balance between these two modes is near equal, and it is entirely natural, even necessary, to convince the top two or three candidates that your organization and this position would be a good place to be.

On the hospitality side, the best advice is to proceed in a way that is aligned with your organizational culture and budget. Putting candidates up in the finest hotel if you are a homeless shelter, or feeding them 16-ounce steaks if you are a hunger alliance, is worse than mere irony. You, of course, want to be generous with candidates and make them feel special. You can do that on a reasonable budget with family restaurants, bed and breakfasts, and interview refreshments. The important thing is that they come away feeling well-treated, well-respected, and, in general, appropriately cared for in a manner that matches the culture of your organization.

Regarding introductions, here are the questions to consider. Is the board's preference for a social mixer or a situation that permits questions and answers? Do the two or three finalists meet the staff or not? Who are the key stakeholders they should meet? What other community officials or leaders should they meet? What kind of an introductory tour of your city should they get?

In general our experience is that, if the finalists are to meet the staff, it happens best at an informal reception versus a question-and-answer session. What you do with staff and how you do it should signal that you do want them in the know, but that, finally, they are not the ones to participate in the decision. With stakeholders, no doubt, you have a particularly enthusiastic donor who would make a positive impression or a foundation official who thinks well of your work. Clearly, what you are going for here are those who will bolster your case that this is a good place to be.

The mayor, city council members, the chamber director, neighborhood leaders, and corporate executives are all people who not only can potentially speak well of you, but well of the city. Also, a physical introduction to the city—from downtown to neighborhoods, suburbs to arts districts, on foot and in the car—is appropriate and helpful. This of course, together with the other introductions, is crucial for out-of-town candidates and mostly optional for any who have already lived and worked in your community. Each candidate from out of town should spend at least one night and parts of two days. With luck, you have a committee member or two who is a natural for this kind of social directing and networking. At this final stage, these are issues that deserve thought and attention.

The Final Decision

Ideally, of course, committee members would come to a unanimous decision. Generally, if there is a sizeable minority (20% or more) who object or a very vocal smaller minority who have a contrary opinion, there is more work to be done. You may need more conversation within the committee, more review of notes from the application and initial interviews, or perhaps more conversation with a candidate or two. That will be a bit of a challenge, but a necessary step, in order to present to the board someone about whom you can be enthusiastic.

Careful attention to dissenters within the committee is important. They may very well have seen, heard, or felt something from a candidate that makes them uncomfortable. If so, the others should ask for more clarification ("What do you see that I don't?"). Sometimes an issue causing resistance can be communicated to the candidate so that he may address it directly. And sometimes, unfortunately, the process gets stalled. Bringing the board in on it for advice may help. Consider bringing in a trusted and highly regarded leader in the nonprofit community who may be able to negotiate out whatever differences remain. Our own experience is that, by paying respectful attention to any dissenters, by reviewing the notes on that candidate from the initial application forward, by bringing any reservation directly to the candidate, or by bringing in the outside assistance of the board or a trusted advisor, the overwhelming majority of differences can be resolved, leading to a mutually respected decision on the part of the search committee.

With, of course, the candidate's assent and pending salary and benefit package negotiations, the favored candidate would be presented to the board together with the rationale and supporting materials for this selection. The committee would present as well a brief description and analysis of the one or two runner-up candidates. At this point, assuming the board accepts the recommendation, it takes over the final matters of negotiating a contract.

Chapter VI

The Board:
Final Checks, Formal Contract

You are now down to final matters and no doubt glad that is the case. This chapter will take you from the serious work of reference and background checks to the celebratory introductions of your new executive director. This is the "all's well that ends well" section, and ending this search process well and happily would be our hope for you.

References

First the important issue of reference checks. More often than not this work will be done by the search committee. Sometimes it is done in collaboration with the board. We assume you know how very important reference checks can be. Our own experience is that they can provide insightful information that will help you better understand your candidate's experience, abilities and style. They can assist in the clarification of specifics noted on a resume or communicated during the interview process. They can serve as a check on the details of job history and responsibilities. And, they can also help you understand the degree to which the candidate is a good match with the culture of your organization.

References can be conducted after the finalists have gone through the majority of the interview process. This allows the reference checks to be utilized to explore questions that surface during the interview process. Regardless of when you decide to do reference checks, remember to get the permission of the candidate to proceed. This is best in writing and can be combined with permission to conduct a background check.

Usually, a candidate will have provided a list of professional and personal references. Individuals who are not listed by a candidate but who have worked with them may be contacted if approved by the candidate. Conducting unauthorized reference checks can jeopardize the integrity of the search process, risk a candidate's confidentiality and damage the trust between those involved in this final process.

When reference checks are being conducted for more than one candidate, stick with the same number for all finalists. References who have worked with a candidate in a professional capacity will likely be more helpful than relatives or friends. Include a variety of reporting relationships to the candidate when selecting references. For example, you might talk with a former supervisor of the candidate, a professional peer, someone who reported to the candidate, a prior board member who worked with the candidate, etc. This provides the board with a variety of perspectives on the candidates.

As with most things, not everyone will be adept at reference checking. Consider who will be best at being able to elicit relevant information through thoughtful and planned questions. This needs to be done with a high level of sensitivity and the strictest of confidence. The information gathered from the references should be accurately summarized and appropriately shared with the committee to offer additional information about the person's qualifications together with clarification about issues raised during the interviews.

Sample Reference Questions:

- Please share the nature and length of your relationship with the candidate.
- Can you describe the role and major responsibilities held by the candidate?
- Are you aware of the candidate's interest in this position or do you have knowledge as to why the candidate is considering a change in organizations?
- What leadership characteristics are most admired in this candidate?
- What are the strongest managerial skills demonstrated by this candidate?
- Describe this candidate's communication style.
- Describe this candidate's decision-making style.
- How would you characterize the candidate's approach to budgeting and finance?
- Do you consider this candidate to be more of an operational manager or more of a visionary?
- What is the nature of the relationship of the candidate with the community?
- Do funders respect and have allegiance to this candidate?
- The board of our organization would like to continually challenge its leader with professional development opportunities. What management or leadership skills would you suggest this candidate work to enhance?

Background Screening

A thorough background investigation will assist in reducing the risk of hiring an individual who has been involved in criminal or other illegal activities. Most all executives will have access to the funds and financial information of the organization. It is critical that your candidate has not been involved in fraud, theft, and/or embezzlement.

Pre-employment screening for your executive position might include:

- Validation of social security number for employment eligibility
- Validation of driver's license and bureau of motor vehicle history
- Validation of (federal and state) professional certifications and/or licenses
- Educational verification
- Employment verification
- Thorough criminal background history
- Credit history
- Fingerprinting and substance abuse screen (based on organizational policy)

You may want to make use of a qualified and reputable expert in the conduct of background checks. To select a competent and reliable individual or company to perform the screening, you can check with the National Association of Professional Background Screeners at: www.napbs.com.

The screening can usually be accomplished within 12 – 36 hours depending on the complexity of a candidate's history and can only be conducted with written consent. The candidate's written consent should be secured utilizing an appropriate release provided by the agency conducting the screening. The cost of this service is ordinarily $50 – $250 and is well worth the relatively small cost.

Board Resolution

A board ruling to extend an offer to a selected candidate needs to occur in order to move forward with the hiring of the executive. Hopefully, the selection of the finalist by the board is a unanimous decision. An undisputed selection of an executive is best for all parties involved. It expresses support of the new leader as she begins in a role that will require board cooperation for the many years ahead. Additionally, the staff will respond more positively to the new executive knowing that the board has made a confident decision.

It is important that the decision-making process is participative. All board members should feel comfortable fully expressing their thoughts and opinions as the process comes to a close. If a clear front-runner emerges a decision may be effortless; however, if several highly qualified and/or unique candidates have emerged, complex and emotional discussions can ensue. Trust and respect by all board members is essential throughout the consensus-building process that will ultimately lead to the decision.

If the board is challenged in reaching consensus, it may elect to conduct another round of interviews or seek the perspectives of stakeholders related to the process. Various methods of an objective rating system can be used to arrive at a decision that might lend discipline and focus to the process. Again, consensus by the board for the selected finalist will be a first step in fostering the success of the next leader.

A formal resolution to ratify the board's desire to extend an offer to a specific individual should be prepared, voted upon, and included in the board minutes. Assuming the board approves this resolution, the chair should immediately offer the position to the selected candidate to gain his intended acceptance, assuming there is a mutually agreed-upon offer letter or contract.

The Offer

A clear and well-developed offer letter or contract enhances the successful closure of the search process. The board should designate an individual to handle the process that includes the design, presentation, and negotiation of the offer or contract to the finalist. Usually, the board appoints its chair or the search committee chair to conduct these actions on its behalf.

An offer letter should express the board's intention to support the new leader. It will serve as a tool to assure accountability and establish trust between the new leader and board. We also recommend that a document defining the reporting structure, responsibilities, and role of the executive be included with or referenced in the offer letter or contract.

Salary

The board should specify and approve the salary to be included in the offer or contract. A salary range for negotiation should be established for the individual working with the selected candidate. The board should be familiar with the candidate's current and past salary and benefit history before establishing the salary range for negotiation. Additionally, the board should understand compensation for similarly qualified leaders in a geographically comparable marketplace within the appropriate nonprofit sector. This enables a board to endorse its leader's salary to all stakeholders. Additionally, it assists in the retention of the leader by ensuring that their salary is competitive with other like-organizations' executives. Salary comparisons can be easily accessed for nonprofits by referencing their IRS Form 990's filed on guidestar.org.

In addition to a specified base salary, compensation might include a bonus and/or incentive component subject to the attainment of defined goals. These should be mutually agreed upon by the board and the executive and relate to the strategic objectives of the organization. The new leader and the board can establish goals at the time of hire or at a later date when there is a clear sense of priorities for the organization.

Benefits

To complement the salary, numerous benefits can be offered to the executive. Benefits should be aligned with the standards that have been set for the organization. A detailed list of potential benefits for your review is included in Chapter IV, page 33.

Noteworthy Inclusions for Your Offer Letter

Noted below are a variety of suggested themes and clauses to consider for inclusion in a letter or contract of employment. These serve to provide clear and concise communication in writing related to a range of issues. Review of the offer letter or contract by legal counsel is strongly recommended prior to presentation to the candidate.

> *"This offer assumes that you will join our organization in a full-time capacity not later than mm/dd/yy."*

> *"Your performance will be reviewed annually on the anniversary of your employment date. You will meet with the board, the executive committee or their designee to review and discuss mutually agreed-upon goals and objectives. A performance review is not a promise of an increase in salary; however, a compensation adjustment will be considered based on your performance, the organization's performance, and economic factors."*

> *"The full extent of your benefits is defined in the employee handbook. You will be requested to sign a document verifying your receipt of the organizational handbook."*

"The board allows you the right to consult and engage in approved outside activities that are communicated in writing prior to their initiation."

"This offer and your employment are conditional upon the satisfactory completion of a background check and references. Additionally, in order to comply with the Immigration Reform and Control Act of 1986, it will be necessary for you to provide documentation verifying your employment eligibility."

"To accept this offer and the terms of this letter, please sign and date on the lines below prior to mm/dd/yy."

"Please sign and date a copy of the attached non-solicitation agreement."

(See Appendix I for sample offer letter.)

Presentation, Negotiation, and Acceptance of the Offer

Presentation

It is acceptable to present an offer in person, via email, or by mail. Ordinarily a conversation has occurred and the disclosure that an offer is forthcoming has been shared. When presenting an offer, review each component of the compensation and benefits package so the recipient has the opportunity to ask for clarification of the terms. It allows the presenter to listen to and discern the candidate's reactions to the terms of the agreement. It's helpful to understand areas most important to the candidate in terms of her priorities and considerations related to acceptance of the offer.

Negotiation

Negotiation may be able to be avoided with a clear understanding of the candidate's current salary and benefits, desired compensation, and the salary range for this position in the marketplace. The board should provide guidance, in terms of negotiation, to the person appointed to present the offer. He should know know where he can be flexible in the negotiation should one develop. If unusual benefits are requested or a salary desired that is beyond the range designated, the negotiator should clearly understand the priorities and importance of these requests. Discussion with the board is necessary if the requests are beyond the scope of the negotiator's authority. Prompt response to these requests is best so that the negotiation can be timely and closure can occur as soon as possible.

Negotiation is also applicable when a counter offer from the candidate's current employer emerges. When you present an offer to a candidate, ask how she'd react to a potential counter- offer; this prompts the candidate's thinking before the situation occurs and can help you gauge her loyalty to your offer. You hope she us prepared to decline a counter-offer; however, should the candidate struggle with a decision related to a counter-offer it's important to understand why. While you may be able to match the counter, you want to make certain a "bidding war" does not evolve. If communication throughout the process has been open, honest, frequent, and timely, a situation like this or a declined offer is more likely to be avoided.

Acceptance

Acceptance of an offer can be verbal initially, but should not be celebrated until the candidate's signature is on the offer document. At this point a new relationship begins and communication with your new leader should intensify. He will, most likely, need to resign a current position, so support at this time is critical to avoid any change of heart. Notes and calls from board members to congratulate the executive are appropriate and encouraged.

Announcement of the New Leader

Once an offer has been accepted, the offer letter or contract has been signed and returned, and the selected candidate has successfully resigned her preceding role (if applicable), you will want to communicate the news publicly in several important steps. These steps, outlined below, are central to a successful introduction of a new leader and provide opportunities for increased exposure to the organization as a result of this major transition. We have found that following these steps in order will make for a smoother and better transition.

Communication to Finalists

Notify all finalists by phone, and later in writing, of the board's selection of another candidate. Thoughtful contact to these individuals enhances the reputation of the board and allows the alternate candidates to hear first-hand they were not selected rather than reading an announcement of the hire in a publication. It is, most likely, inappropriate to share the name of the selected candidate at this time since staff and key stakeholders may not yet have been notified of the selection.

Candidates who are current or prior board members, or internal associates at the organization who were in consideration for the position, should be contacted first in the notification process. These individuals should be treated with special care as they will, hopefully, remain a part of the ongoing life of the organization.

Communication to Staff

Next, share and introduce information about the new leader to the management and staff of the organization. A search process can stir interest and curiosity within any environment, and the sooner the staff is notified of the hire, the better. Staff members should not hear the news about the new executive from anyone other than the board.

Communication to Key Stakeholders

Nonprofits may have key stakeholders who deserve notification of or introduction to the new leader prior to an announcement to the general public. These may be significant donors, major funders, politicians, etc. The board might consider making calls or personal visits to these stakeholders to share the good news. At some future date, a reception to introduce the new leader might be appropriate.

Press Release

A press release announcing the hire of a new leader is an important tool to initiate public relations opportunities for the organization. It can be shared with local media and publications, and, when applicable, select regional or national publications in the field. The press release should be concise, factual, and interesting. The following is a simple format that might be utilized.

Mary Jones Named Executive Director of the ABC Coalition
Columbus, Ohio
<DATE>

The Board of the ABC Coalition announced that Mary Jones has been named Executive Director.

<Quote from Board representative>

Mary Jones comes to ABC from the XYZ Center, which has provided family services to the Central Ohio area for 130 years. Jones joined the XYZ Center as Director in 2005. During her tenure with XYZ, Jones also served as the National Chairperson for the National Coalition for Children's Issues.

Ms. Jones will begin her new role in July.

ABC Coalition is a non-profit community based organization. Located in Columbus, Ohio, ABC has been serving Franklin County families since 1950. For more information call (614) 123-4567 or go to www.ABCcoalition.org.

Chapter VII

The First 100 Days for the Board and New Executive

It may not be exactly 100 days. It may be 120 or 90 or some other number that you determine. The point is that there is a crucial start-up period for a new executive that requires a special kind of attention. The board may decide that it is its job to do, or ask, the search committee to take responsibility for this initial phase in the relationship between new executive and the organization. Sometimes, the board will appoint a special transition committee comprised of board and search committee members to attend to this important time period. The transition work does not conclude with the hiring. The board needs to see that the ongoing and special work of the first 100 days does get the kind of attention it deserves. However you choose to proceed thinking about and acting upon these matters should be done jointly with the new executive; hence, this chapter is for both of you.

Four matters to consider. We will first look at what tends to make for success in this new relationship. Secondly, we will outline some ways to begin working in partnership. Third, the other relationships with staff, stakeholders, and the past executive director will then be considered. And finally, we will respond to the challenge of managing the work and planning for evaluation.

An Agenda for Success

From our experience, three main factors influence the success of the early transition period for the new executive: familiarity, listening, and match. A word about each.

Familiarity. The extent of knowledge about the organization that the new director has before beginning his work.

The new executive has much to become acquainted with in an organization: staff, board, constituents, programs, and administrative procedures and policies, to name a few. Prior knowledge of these greatly affects the learning curve and the new executive's ability to fully engage and lead. Sometimes coming to the organization fresh without prior biases has advantages, but overall familiarity with the people and mission of the organization makes for a shorter and smoother transition period.

Listening. The time the new director takes to understand before making changes.

Starting right off with a lot of action steps and change strategies probably would not be well-received. Organizations do respond well to movement and progress, but they respond far better if the progress is thoughtful and considered. It is fine—even important – for a new director to assemble a new vision for the organization; the operative word here is assemble. That implies hearing from and taking in the insights and hopes of the key constituents to fully understand the situation. That will not easily be done in less than 100 days. One successor we spoke with said it took over six months to feel comfortable putting a personal stamp on any part of the organization, while another felt that even several years after the transition there were new things to learn. So keep in mind that while a new director should not take a passive approach to leading, the new executive should keep listening well into her tenure.

Match. The degree to which the new director already embodies the key aspects of the organization's culture.

This is a subtle one and not easily described. "Match" is roughly what we mean when we say, "Anne is a natural for that job." It has to do with fit, affinity, or confluence—the ease with which people can look at the leader and look at the organization and see the match. Leaders who quickly and naturally embody the mission within themselves and who represent the organizational essence in the community have an extra-special strength and validity. When an organization can find such a person who also has the set of abilities the job requires, a distinctive confluence occurs that makes for effectiveness as a leader.

John Gabarro, in an excellent book, *The Dynamics of Taking Charge* (publisher/year?), outlines a longer transition period than 100 days and claims that five important components are essential to a successful start-up period. They are:

1. *Taking hold* – a period of orientation and evaluative learning and corrective action.

2. *Immersion* – a period of relatively little change but more reflective and penetrating learning.

3. *Reshaping* – a period of major change during which the new manager acts on the deeper understanding gained in the preceding stage.

4. *Consolidation* – a period in which earlier stages are consolidated.

5. *Refinement* – a period of fine-tuning and relatively little major additional learning.

Gabarro goes on to say that as a result of his own research he found that the big difference between the successful and failed transitions had to do with the quality of the new executive's relationships at the end of the first year. Three out of four of the failures had poor relationships with two or more of their key subordinates, and all had poor working relationships with their superiors (the board).

We include this work of Gabarro because even though it was done in the private sector it is so similar to our own experiences with transitions in the nonprofit sector. We respond especially to the vital importance of establishing positive relationships in the early stages of the transition. And so, we turn to surely the most crucial relationship—that with the board of directors.

Try not to spend a lot of time debating just whose responsibility it is to initiate the new partnership. The new executive will get the message that a genuine partnership is what the board devises if the board takes a strong initiative in getting the executive properly introduced around the organization and around the community. This kind of action on the part of the board signals to the new executive that "we too plan to lead and take responsibility…you are not in this alone." While in the course of final interviews the executive (then-finalist) did receive certain important introductions, no doubt other important ones need to be made. The board should take the time with individual members to see that it gets done with the right mix of professionalism and personality. It does not all have to happen in the first two weeks—the executive has other matters to attend to—but it should probably happen over the first six to eight weeks. Key people will want to meet the new executive, and the executive will want to begin the work of building relationships with them.

Sometimes the best way to form a strong partnership between the board and the executive is for the board president to initiate conversations about matters of clear mutual interest. Here are four that the two of you may wish to have over the early weeks of the transition.

1. *A conversation about goals.* Not only will the executive have goals, the board president can and should have some as well. Share those goals. Note the similarities that will strengthen your work together. Note also the goals that are different. They too can enlarge or strengthen your work together and your impact on the rest of the board.

2. *A conversation about tone and style.* Try another conversation about the kind of organizational tone and style the two of you want to create. Maybe it includes the permission to ask more questions, and even to challenge reports and proposals. Or maybe you wish to ensure that more time is spent on big issues and less energy given over to small details. Perhaps holding prompt and productive meetings and maneuvering through an efficient agenda is what you want. Whatever the special environmental condition you wish to bring about, merely announcing it won't make it happen. The two of you need to embody it, model it for the rest of the leaders, and see that it happens in practice.

3. *A conversation about what to avoid.* Try a conversation about what you want to avoid – not obvious things like misunderstandings, but more specific things like private conversations in board meetings while business is being conducted, or surprising the other with a new proposal in a board meeting. You may also want to avoid having too-full agendas, re-discussing and re-deciding an issue, allowing any one or two board members to dominate a discussion, or creating structure and practice by which the executive committee becomes the in-group, the quasi-board. You no doubt will have your own favorite list of things you don't want to happen.

4. *A conversation about board meeting preparation.* Try yet another conversation about all the issues that surround board meetings—the before, during, and after tasks that one or the other of you will inherit. Following is a list of some examples that executives and board presidents divide in different ways:

1. Writing the meeting announcement reminder

2. Telephoning special people to get them there

3. Seeing that minutes are ready for presentation

4. Creating the agenda

5. Writing the agenda for distribution

6. Arranging the meeting space

7. Arranging the refreshments, if any

8. Making sure minutes are taken and checked

9. Thanking special guests

10. Inquiring about members not present

The focus here is getting the partnership between the new executive and board president off to a good start. That can model the broader partnership between the full board and the executive.

Yet another way to build the executive-board partnership in the early stage of the transition is for the board and the executive to fully understand the special challenges each faces during this time, and to be of assistance to one another in addressing these challenges.

John Tebbe in *Transition Guides* mentions several important early challenges for both executive and board. The executive's early challenges include:

- Gaining an understanding of the organization and acquiring knowledge—quickly.

- Figuring out "who's who" and establishing solid working relationships.

- Setting good priorities.

- Meeting pent-up demands for change and decisions that may have been deferred during the interim period.

- Managing expectations and negotiating competing demands.

- Building a support coalition to back the changes she may have identified.

- Balancing both organizational and personal transitions, which can be a challenge to maintaining personal equilibrium and well-being.

Similarly, the board faces its own set of early challenges:

- Shifting gears after the search and finding the energy to address the important relationship-building work.

- Effectively launching and supporting its new executive.

- Adjusting to the new executive's leadership style as well as his expectations and needs from the board.

- Attending to the trust-building phase.

- Avoiding the dangerous polarities of micromanagement and excessive confidence.

- Avoiding "savior thinking" and dealing with buyer's remorse.

- Ensuring that legacy issues and "thinking ruts" don't derail this work.

You may identify more particular challenges that exist in your situation. In forming a strong beginning partnership, perhaps nothing is of more importance than clear awareness of one another's special challenges and a desire to address them fully.

Relationship Tending

Much of what relationship tending means around stakeholders and staff is self evident. While the new executive may here be the one in the lead, the board can assist with determining the priorities and character of that lead. Perhaps the first and best perspective here is that interactions with stakeholders and staff are not interruptions of the work; they are part of the work. Sometimes executives lose sight of that perspective when they are hard at work on a budget or a memo. With stakeholders, apart from initiating and nurturing relationships, it is keeping them informed about progress and supplying any specialized information any of them need. It is also being sensitive to the fact that they do not all need and want the same kind and amount of information and the same kind and amount of attention.

Staff members first are curious and want to know who this executive is—what this new person cares about and plans to do. Those who were candidates for the executive position will require special attention. Tending to staff at this early stage might also include:

- Understanding what they like about working here

- Exploring their own hopes and goals for the organization

- Becoming familiar with their career plans

- Getting their perspective on the organization challenges and issues

- Understanding the previous pattern and purposes of staff meetings

- Identifying what additional opportunities and experiences they would like within the organization

- Checking with them for additional important individual and organizational contacts

- Discussing and agreeing upon a schedule of individual meetings with them

- Discerning the history of staff evaluations and discuss what now would be helpful and appropriate

The new executive's relationship with the past executive can be useful to non-existent. It does depend on so many matters. For now, let us assume the past executive is around and in good health, and departed in an amicable manner. If all that is true, read on. If not, skip ahead to the next section.

The nature of the past executive's ongoing relationship with the staff, board, and new director is not a simple matter. We have experienced a variety of scenarios. The key in all of them seemed to be that the new director—not the past one—was the primary determiner of the who, how, and when of this. One new director utilized the previous one as a paid personal consultant for six months. In another the previous director departed to an out-of-state position and had little or no contact.

For the previous director this is the leadership of letting go, of getting on with life, of permitting the organization to go forward in new ways and with new leadership—out from under the watchful eyes. The leadership of letting go is likely not an easy challenge after years of shepherding an organization and building personal relationships. However, all of the evidence suggests that letting go and allowing the new executive to be the guide in terms of any ongoing involvement is the strategy that will best serve the organization.

Further, any new executive will rather quickly discover what the strengths of the previous leader were and exactly what had been done less well. Without question the new executive will inherit things that need at least management attention and perhaps fixing or solving. The fixing and solving categories require time and effort not readily available given all else the executive needs to learn and do. The obvious temptation is to be critical of the previous director for not having tended to these issues. Such criticism, if widely expressed, is likely to have a larger and more negative effect on the organization's assessment of the new executive, rather than its assessment of the recently departed executive. Not a good start. Such criticisms and "what to do about it" conversations are best relegated to the privacy of trusted confidants.

Managing the Work, Planning for Executive Evaluation

Most executives who have held a position or two know how to set goals and design work plans. And, most boards have lived through a variety of good and not-so-good ways of planning work. For either party, the setting of goals and establishing of short-term plans is likely not to be new business. What is new is that this particular executive and this particular board have not done it together. As a result, early conversations about what has been our usual way are important. That, of course, should transition quickly into how can we now build upon the separate good and bad experiences to formulate our own new together way of proceeding.

A note for the board: Depending on which study you read, 60 to 70% of executives have received no regular evaluation. So, not only is experience with this part of the work thin to nil, evaluation is a far more sensitive and personal endeavor than developing goals and planning for work. On this one, we will refer you to a small book and give you a bit more right here. The book is *Evaluating Your Executive: New Approaches, New Purposes* (see For Additional Reading). Here, then, is a bit more.

First, set the tone for executive evaluation. Too many executives come away from their evaluation experience feeling less competent, less powerful, less confident, and more confused about what is expected of them. Any one of those is not a good thing and taken together they are very much not a good thing.

What we know about ourselves is that when, for whatever reason, we are lacking in confidence and unsure of ourselves and our abilities, we do not perform very well. What we of course want for our leaders is that they will want to try, believing they can do yet better and wishing to overcome whatever barriers may stand in the way of the mission to which they and the organization are committed. That is the tone you want in your executive evaluation experience—one that produces energy and positive forward action rather than results that are draining, tiring, and weakening. Most all of us know and feel the difference and have, in fact, experienced it in our own lives. The challenge is to recreate this energy in the experience of executive evaluation.

Perhaps, then, the ultimate test of the success of your executive evaluation is whether or not the executive comes away feeling clearer and more confident about your expectations; stronger and better able to face the unavoidable challenges in the life of your organization; more inspired to learn and grow professionally; and more appreciative and trusting in the relationship among all those responsible for the leadership of your organization.

Second, clarify expectations for the evaluation. You and your executive may wish to choose agenda items for your pre-evaluation conversation from the following:

1. What purposes do the board and the executive believe the evaluation should serve?

2. How will we decide which inventory/process to utilize?

3. What is the right balance between executive self-evaluation and committee evaluation of the executive?

4. To what extent will this be a conversation-based review?

5. To what extent will some form of rating be made on each item prior to a conversation?

6. What experiences about evaluation do each of us bring to this evaluation experience?

7. What are some of the things we would wish to avoid?

What this list suggests to us is that the pre-evaluation conversation is crucial, will take time and thought, and, if done right, will go a long way toward ensuring a satisfactory executive evaluation experience.

Finally, all evaluations serve purposes, whether intended or not. We believe that two of the more important purposes are for professional development and to strengthen the collegiality between the executive and the board.

It would be difficult to find arguments against professional development for an executive. Still, too many miss the opportunity to foster that development with executive evaluation. What executive would not want its board to encourage and support her professional development, and what board would not want an executive who was on the lookout for learning? Our experience is that this works best when the board is in a "how can we assist" mode, rather than a "here's what you need to learn and how you ought to do it" mode. In our view, the movement should always be in the direction of self-directed, not other-directed, learning. Executives need to be encouraged to fully graduate from the "teacher knows best" style. As adult learners, executives need to be pointed toward, and encouraged in, a self-reflective process of asking, "What do I need to know and to be able to do and how am I going to learn it?"

Boards can and should participate between the board and executive in identifying an agenda for professional development. They can even assist in structuring it and identifying sources for it. What they probably should not do is take away the executive's initiative and begin to be in charge of the professional education of another adult. In addition, while much professional development can result from reading and informal peer discussion, boards can also see that some funds are made available for professional seminars and conferences.

Strengthening the new partnership with your executive can also be enhanced by the evaluation experience. It is particularly important that the executive and board leadership exemplify a way of being together that they hope will characterize the committee, staff, and volunteer relationships throughout the organization.

As all of us have experienced personally and professionally, such exemplary relationships do not just magically come about. They take work and they take periods of time when that work can get done. One of our executive colleagues says that a part of his job is to see that the board members have a satisfying experience engaged in some-thing of significance to the mission he signed up to hold in trust. We would add that it is also part of the job of the board to see that the executive has a satisfying experience, significantly engaged in the organizational mission he signed up to give his work-life to. That level of attention to the other, in this leadership partnership, sets the stage for things to go well. If part (or even most) of leading is about serving, a board and executive who can get in that serving mode toward one another are going to create the kind of organization where you, and others, want to be.

Back to the first 100 days and to you who are as board members and executives. Our own belief is that if, in your first 100 days, you pay attention to what tends to lead to success, build a strong partnership between executive and board, tend to important relationships, and create good work plans and productive and encouraging ways to evaluate, you will have laid the groundwork for a long, productive, and satisfying partnership.

Afterwords I

Your Succession Plan: Mostly Done

Succession planning is everywhere mentioned and yet seldom practiced these days. Nonprofit organizations hear about it from funders, consultants, and conference speakers. It ranks up there with transparency, metrics, and measurements as things to which we are to pay ardent and immediate attention. So why all the talk, what does it mean, and what is the problem to which it is the answer? And, you might add the very good question: Why would we write about it here?

Let's start with why here. If you have gone carefully through the executive search steps which we have outlined above, you already have fairly well in place four of the five usual components of succession planning (more on the fifth in a few paragraphs). So we would urge you to pull out and summarize the four mostly done, and label it "succession plan," and file it in a memorable and accessible place.

Secondly, like lots of things with somewhat fancy titles, succession planning is a fairly simple concept. What it refers to is a process by which you can have a smooth and orderly transition to new executive leadership. That's it. It is doing that thinking and planning in advance, so you do not have to be in the familiar "what do we do now" mode when your executive announces they are going to leave. It also covers the more dramatic, emergency event, which suddenly leaves you without a leader.

It does seem to be one of those things which boards and executives put somewhere near the bottom of their stack of "to do" items. It is, after all, about tomorrow, and, frankly, most of us have enough to do about today to keep us busy. It also concerns a situation that we would rather not contemplate. Dealing with the issues around a departing executive and anticipating the work of an executive search rather quickly transports us into a "let's worry about that later" mode. But then remember that they who know (and consultants don't always) have pretty good data that, on average, 75% of the executives within our sector will leave their positions within the next five years.

Back to the claim that having gone through the executive search process described in these pages, you have four of the five succession planning components mostly done. Here are the five that most believe to be the core of a succession plan:

1. Full knowledge and understanding of the job of the executive.

2. A plan for interim leadership in an emergency.

3. A pattern and process for executive evaluation.

4. Expectations and roles for the executive and the board.

5. A way for the board to assess its own performance.

If you match these with the executive search work outlined above you will find that 1 is fairly well covered in the executive profile and position description (Chapter III); 2 had been partially addressed in the discussion about an interim director (Chapter II); 3 is quite fully addressed in "the work and the evaluation" during the first 100 days (Chapter VII); 4 is contained in the roles section (Chapter III); and, finally, 5 remains yet to be accomplished, but you as a board could discuss and write up a board self-assessment process that works for you. See Appendix III for an example of how you might do this.

There is a "however" to all this, and that however has to do with the existence of a strategic plan. It is the strategic plan that forms the foundation of the succession plan. and therefore is a part of a total package of documents that are useful to critical in the ongoing life of your organization. Exactly where the succession plan starts and the strategic plan stops is a matter of opinion. Our own take on it is that the strategic plan would focus primarily on understanding and updating the mission; two to four years' worth of goals and objectives; a way of tracking progress on these goals; and full knowledge of the present and future financial realities and plans. Those four items form a strong foundation for a successful succession plan.

Final Thoughts, Parting Words from the Editorial Advisory Committee

The hiring of an executive director is perhaps the most important decision a board can make. A well-chosen executive will successfully advance the agency's agenda for years. This little book provides proven strategies to help you get the most from your recruitment and selection process.
— Jonathan C. Beard, Executive Director

Finding a new executive director to head an organization can be a great time of discovery and rejuvenation for both parties—or a disaster. I think boards for small and larger organizations can benefit greatly from the thoughtful and realistic advice offered in this book to assure the best returns on everyone's efforts. Ultimately your community benefits from a job well done.
— David E. Chesebrough, Executive Director

Hiring a new executive director can seem like a daunting task. But, have hope. The Search Book: A Guide to Executive Selection *provides a framework and "how to" guide for the executive search. Both small and large organizations will benefit from knowing how to think about the process, whether you are conducting the search yourselves or using an outside firm.*
— Ann S. Hoaglin, Board President

As time-consuming as it may seem to follow the advice set forth in this publication, more difficult will be living day-to-day with the results of a hasty and poorly made decision. Do it right by following the guidance contained in this publication. You will find the right executive director for your organization, and you'll have some fun and develop your organization at the same time.
— Annette Houck, Labor and Employment Law Attorney

To do an effective executive search requires the best from all of us within the organization. Our work is too important not to do it well. Our work is too hard not to learn together. Our work is too meaningful not to share it with each other.

— Cynthia Lazarus, Executive Director

When you first learn that your Executive is leaving, your initial reaction may be one of fear or panic. Remember to maintain a positive perspective and view the search process as an opportunity to reassess your organizational needs and to reexamine what type of leader is needed to continue to move the work of the organization forward. Staying focused and on track will undoubtedly lead you to a successful outcome that will benefit all stakeholders.

— Dawn Tyler Lee, Board President

Not-for-profit organizations are the backbone of the delivery of social service amenities to communities. Therefore it is absolutely essential for the progress of the social service sector to attract and retain exceptional talent to enhance the delivery of services in the areas of education, health, and welfare. The executive search process for not-for-profit organizations is both an art and a science; it must be flexible and concrete. The execution of a successful search is evident when all parties feel that they have recruited the right executive to advance the mission of the organization.

— Debra Plousha Moore, Board President

Take the time to conduct a thoughtful, well-planned search. A rigorous organizational assessment and a thorough executive profile will advance the organization and its mission as well as help you hire the right executive director.

— Susan D. Rector, Board President

❦

Much will be said about the executive you choose. Their ultimate successes, failures, strengths and shortcomings will be the focus of many conversations in a variety of circles. Be sure that the same or greater levels of conversation and deliberation are employed as you recruit, interview, and select the person to lead your organization's strides toward greatness. This book serves as a great resource to help ensure your success.

— Mataryun "Mo" Wright, Board Development Consultant

Additional Resources

Adams, Richard, Shirley Magoteaux, Virginia Matz, Cheryl Stiefel-Francis, Judy Westerheide with Donn F. Vickers. *The Board Member's Guide: Making a Difference on Your Board and in Your Community.* Columbus: The Academy for Leadership & Governance, 2003.

Albert, Sheila. *Hiring the Chief Executive.* Washington, D.C.: BoardSource, 2000.

Axelrod, Nancy R. *Chief Executive Succession Planning.* Washington, D.C.: BoardSource, 2002.

Bell, Jeanne, Richard Moyers, and Tim Wolfred. *Daring to Lead 2006: A National Study of Nonprofit Leadership.* San Francisco: CompassPoint (and the Meyer Foundation), 2006.

Boyett, Joseph, and Jimmie Boyett. *The Guru Guide: The Best Ideas of the Top Management Thinkers.* New York: Wiley, 1998.

Collins, Jim. *Good to Great and the Social Sector.* Boulder: Collins, 2005.

CompassPoint Nonprofit Service. Homepage. www.compasspoint.org.

Drucker, Peter. *The Essential Drucker: The Best of Sixty Years of Peter Drucker's Essential Writings on Management.* New York: HarperCollins Publishers, 2003.

Gabarro, John J. *The Dynamics of Taking Charge.* Cambridge: Harvard Business School Press, 1987.

Illinois Arts Alliance. Homepage. www.artsalliance.org.

Kouzes, James M., and Barry Z. Posner. *Leadership Challenge: The Five Practices of Exemplary Leadership.* San Francisco: Jossey-Bass, 2002.

Succession: Arts Leadership for the 21st Century. Chicago: Illinois Arts Alliance/ Foundation, 2003.

Tebbe, John. *The Post-Hire Phase: Launching a Thriving Relationship.* TransitionGuides, v. 2, n. 2004. Retrieved March 20, 2007 from http://www.transitionguides.com/newsltr/TL_2_2.htm#feature

Vickers, Donn F. and Kelly Stevelt Kaser. *Evaluating Your Executive: New Approaches, New Purposes.* Columbus: The Academy for Leadership & Governance, 2006.

Wolfred, Tim. *Interim Executive Directors: The Power in the Middle.* Baltimore: The Annie E. Casey Foundation, 2005.

Appendix I

Sample Position Descriptions for the Executive Director

Position Description I

The Executive Director is the Chief Executive Officer of [organization]. The Executive Director reports to the Board of Directors and is responsible for the organization's consistent achievement of its mission and financial objectives.

In program development and administration, the Executive Director will:

1. Assure that the organization has a long-range strategy which achieves its mission and toward which it makes consistent and timely progress.

2. Provide leadership in developing program, organizational, and financial plans with the Board of Directors and staff, and carry out plans and policies authorized by the board.

3. Promote active and broad participation by volunteers in all areas of the organization's work.

4. Maintain official records and documents, and ensure compliance with federal, state, and local regulations.

5. Maintain a working knowledge of significant developments and trends in the field.

In communications, the Executive Director will:

1. See that the board is kept fully informed on the condition of the organization and all important factors influencing it.

2. Publicize the activities of the organization, its programs and goals.

3. Establish sound working relationships and cooperative arrangements with community groups and organizations.

4. Represent the programs and point of view of the organization to agencies, organizations, and the general public.

In relations with staff, the Executive Director will:

1. Be responsible for the recruitment, employment, and release of all personnel, both paid staff and volunteers.

2. Ensure that job descriptions are developed, that regular performance evaluations are held, and that sound human resource practices are in place.

3. See that an effective management team, with appropriate provision for succession, is in place.

4. Encourage staff and volunteer development and education, and assist program staff in relating their specialized work to the total program of the organization.

5. Maintain a climate that attracts, keeps, and motivates a diverse staff of top-quality people.

In budget and finance, the Executive Director will:

1. Be responsible for developing and maintaining sound financial practices.

2. Work with the staff, finance committee, and the board in preparing a budget; see that the organization operates within budget guidelines.

3. Ensure that adequate funds are available to permit the organization to carry out its work.

4. Jointly with the president and secretary of the board of directors, prepare official correspondence of the organization, and, jointly with designated officers, executive legal documents.

Note: Many national and local organizations are willing to share their ED job descriptions with others. It's worth a call or two to friends on other boards to see if they have good ones to share… or to encourage them to develop a job description if there isn't a recent one in place!

Position Description II

The Executive Director is responsible for the leadership and management of [organization], a nonprofit organization that exists to [mission statement]. The organization provides the following services: [specify]. The Executive Director reports to and works in partnership with a board of directors and is responsible for developing and managing the organization's [size of] budget, supervising a paid staff of [size]. The salary range is [$ to $]. The following benefits are provided: [specify].

Qualifications and Characteristics:

- Minimum of five years' experience working in a nonprofit organization, including supervising staff and working with a board of directors;
- Academic degree and/or extensive experience in [mission area of nonprofit organization];
- Working knowledge of nonprofit fiscal management, including fund accounting and budgeting;
- Demonstrated ability in public speaking, written and oral communication, and interpersonal relations;
- Experience in fundraising; and,
- Maturity and high level of energy.

Responsibilities:

- Oversee all programs, services, and activities to ensure that program objectives are met;

- Develop office and personnel policies;

- Conduct searches and appoint staff;

- Help board chair plan agendas and develop background materials for meetings of the board of directors;

- Facilitate a regular strategic planning process;

- Prepare an annual budget to be approved by the board of directors;

- Approve expenditures;

- Work with the board and staff to raise funds from outside sources; and,

- Serve as chief liaison with other community organizations and key constituent groups.

This description was contained in a small book well worth reading: *Hiring the Chief Executive* (BoardSource, 2000).

Appendix II

Sample Offer Letter

<Date>

<Candidate Name>
<Address>

Dear **<Candidate>**,

It is my pleasure to extend this offer of employment to you for **<position title>** with **<organization name>**. As **<position title>,** your primary responsibilities will include **<short description of job responsibilities>.** I extend this offer, and the opportunity it represents with great confidence in your abilities. You will report to me, **<title of person role reports to>.**

The terms of this offer of employment are as follows:

Start Date	This offer assumes that you will join **<organization name>** in a full-time capacity on **<date>.**
Annual Base Salary	Your base salary will be **$<salary>** annually.
Bonus Compensation	You will be eligible to receive a bonus up to **<xx>%** of your base salary. This additional compensation will be determined by your achievement of mutually agreed-upon individual and organizational goals set by the Board. Additionally, a bonus will only be considered if our organization's financial status is positive.
Annual Review	Your performance and base salary will be reviewed annually. A base salary adjustment and potential bonus compensation will be based on both your performance and other factors that might include economic conditions and organization well-being.

Benefits	**Defined below are the benefits as offered by the organization:**
	Health Insurance
	Vision Insurance
	Dental Insurance
	Short-Term Disability
	Long-Term Disability
	Life Insurance
	Vacation
	Sick Leave
	Personal Days
	Holidays
	Retirement Plan
	Miscellaneous

<May include items such as cell phone allowance, vehicle allowance, computer, tuition reimbursement, cafeteria/flexible benefit options, professional development, license fees, parking, membership in associations or clubs, journal subscriptions>

This offer and your employment with **<organization name>** are conditional upon the satisfactory completion of a background check, substance screening, and references. Additionally, this offer is based on your representation that you are under no legal impediment to accept this offer and perform the anticipated services. In order to comply with the Immigration Reform and Control Act of 1986, it will be necessary for you to provide documentation verifying your employment eligibility. Although your employment will be at-will and this offer does not create a contract of employment or employment for a specified term, it is my hope that your acceptance of this offer will be just the beginning of a mutually beneficial relationship with **<organization name>.**

Upon acceptance of this offer, we ask that you sign, date and return one of the two letters in the enclosed envelope. This offer remains outstanding until end of day **<expiration date>.**

<Name>, we are excited about the possibilities of your joining our team. I look forward to working with you as we continue the successful growth of **<organization name>.**

Sincerely,

ACCEPTANCE:
To accept this offer and the terms of this letter, please sign and date below prior to **<expiration date>.**

Offer accepted:

_____ _____

<Candidate Name>   **<Date>**

Appendix III

Sample Board Self-Assessment Tool

     This method may work best in the form of an outline completed by individual board members and then discussed individually with the board president or chair of the nominating committee. The goal is to assist board members not only in becoming more involved, but also in becoming more appropriately involved. These questions—either sent out to board members or used as part of a reflective time at a board meeting (with responses collected on the spot)—may assist you in better utilizing the resources of your board membership.

Inventory of Board Member Participation

1. In the upcoming year on the board I would like to take personal responsibility for _____.

2. I would be willing to have further conversation about being considered for the following offices and committee chair positions (circle one):

   President   Vice President   Secretary   Treasurer

   List your committees: _____

   _____

   _____

   _____

   _____

3. My previous board involvement has been mostly _____.
   I would like to move toward _____.

4. A new effort I think is important for our organization and that I would like to help with is _____.

5. A task I particularly enjoy at work or home that I have yet to do on this board is _____.

6. My most treasured board experience has to do with _____.

7. I would consider this upcoming year a success if the board was able to

   _____.